COMPLEX FOOTBALL

From Seirul·lo´s Structured Training

To Frade´s Tactical Periodisation

"The man with a new idea is a crank until the idea succeeds"

Mark Twain

Complex Football

First published in Spain in 2015 by Topprosoccer S.L.

Copyright: Javier Mallo Sainz © 2015

All rights reserved. Javier Mallo Sainz has asserted his rights to be identified as the author of this work.

No part of this publication may be reproduced, stored in any electronic format or other retrieval system, or transmitted, in any form or by any means, electronical, mechanical, photocopying, recording or otherwise, without the prior permission of the copyright owner.

Author: Javier Mallo Sainz

Final English review: Archit Navandar

1st Edition - August 2015

ISBN: 978-84-606-9666-7

D.L.: M-004416/2015

www.complexfootball.com

CONTENTS

FOREWORD *by Pedro Marques* 7

FOREWORD *by Rafael Martín Acero* 10

FOREWORD *by Xavier Tamarit* 13

INTRODUCTION 17

PART I: THE NEED FOR A PARADIGM SHIFT IN SCIENCE AND FOOTBALL 23

I.1 Traditional approach to football training 25

    I.1.1 Foundations of sports training 25

    I.1.2 The influence of Classical Thinking on the theory and practice of sports training 27

    I.1.3 New directions to study team sports 38

I.2 The Paradigm of Complexity in football 42

    I.2.1 Foundations of Complex Thinking 43

    I.2.2 Application of Complex Thinking to football 47

PART II: SEIRUL·LO'S STRUCTURED TRAINING 63

II.1 The origin: Paco Seirul·lo 65

II.2 A training methodology based on the person (The footballer) ... 71

    II.2.1 The person and his (self-)structuring as the referential axis of the process 71

    II.2.2 The foundations of Structured Training 76

II.3 Planning in football 81

    II.3.1 Definition of planning 81

    II.3.2 The concept of sporting shape in the footballer 83

    II.3.3 Characteristics of planning in football 86

II.4 The process of Structured Training... 92

    II.4.1 Planning tasks in Structured Training..................................... 93

    II.4.2 Programming tasks in Structured Training.............................. 99

    II.4.3 Design tasks in Structured Training....................................... 110

    II.4.4 Control and Evaluation tasks in Structured Training................. 114

PART III: FRADE´S TACTICAL PERIODIZATION.................................. 117

III.1 Vítor Frade: The father of Tactical Periodization............................. 119

III.2 The Game Model... 123

III.3 Methodological Principles... 133

III.4 The Morphocycle.. 141

    III.4.1 The first week of the season... 144

    III.4.2 The Morphocycle (from the second week of the season on)....... 145

    III.4.3 The Exceptional Morphocycle.. 159

III.5 Tactical Periodization vs traditional training..................................... 162

EPILOGUE.. 167

BIBLIOGRAPHY.. 171

FOREWORD

by Pedro Marques[1]

Football, a passion beyond limits

For most of us it usually starts at early ages, evolves through our lives and is present until our last days. Some of us participate to the football phenomenon by devoting a lot of energy to follow a team - fully hearted - others are fortunate enough to get closer contact through different professional roles within the game or its education. There are a lot of common points between all football lovers, *but what distinguishes them? What makes the difference between the fan in the stand and the coach on the bench?*

The game is evolving on the sidelines

Modern dedicated followers don't look anymore just to watch exciting plays from afar, they look to be part of it, to get more participation and intimately live everything that happens to their team. On this fast paced digital era, the proximity between fans, coaches, teams and players tends to get facilitated and there is a lot more access from outside to coaching insights, to match information and everyday we get contact with clever resources applied in and around the game (e.g. data widgets, video telestrators, infographics). More and more there are many interesting pieces of work created by smart people 'outside' football (e.g. bankers, data architects, neuroscientists), lots of them are not directly involved with a team or needing to win at the weekend, although this doesn't mean they are less important adding dynamic thought to a global and connected movement that pushes new ideas and trends towards the evolution of the game (e.g. analytics advances in recruitment, new writers and bloggers consulted by clubs, pundits using high-tech match analysis support).

---

[1] *Degree in Physical Education Teaching and Sports - Football- & Post-graduation in High Performance Training (Faculty of Human Kinetics, Lisbon, Portugal). Current Global Lead for Football Performance at City Football Group. Former 1st team Performance Analyst at Manchester City FC (2010-2014) and Sporting Clube de Portugal (2004-2010).*

Down to the training ground

At pitch level the game never stops and over the last 30/40 years an increased proximity between the empirical (practical) and scientific (academic) knowledge has allowed it to move at high pace; smarter questions, founded discussions and the development of better training methods lead to improved preparation and performances. The differences at the top-level are even smaller and the capacity to constantly challenge and improve current practices differentiates the good from the best.

Coaches and support staff are the ones responsible for creating the right environments and applying the appropriate methods needed to elevate the individual potential and collective dynamics towards the team's objectives and successes. From within, they are in a privileged position to assess the context and its resources from multiple angles and, as an example, they are the ones with direct and extensive contact with the players and can promote certain behaviours. In the end, coaches and staff dictate the whole preparation leading to the match day: what spaces does that midfielder need to understand and dominate so they can balance the team while in attack? What exercise designs, timings and feedbacks will promote greater levels of learning and auto-organisation so we can press from the front with good coordination? How can we reach the right activation levels in training so it transfers in to a strong start and sustained performance in the game? These are some of the numerous questions that coaches and staff have to be prepared to solve throughout the training week... these clearly go beyond fans' worries as usually their focus is, rightly, on enjoying the 90 minutes after kick-off.

Seirul·lo and Frade: two great influencers

We all know that there are several ways to skin a cat, and the same applies to winning! No, there are no magic formulas. But I believe that those who win considerably more often and more consistently, have something they do differently.

Although the achievement of the perfect game is a utopia, this is what fires the drive to become better everyday. That desire, is translated into constant study of the game and a close relation between practice and multidisciplinary reflection.

Seirul·lo and Frade, via their systematised approaches (going far beyond football knowledge only), developed through the years two different methodologies that surpass the traditional and uni-dimensional views of the game; in unique fashion they integrate different concepts and set new visions for football training allowing its followers to get closer to the essence of this complex game. Always in interaction with the game itself, players and coaches, their contributions are all-round, robust and worth understanding.

Although I never had the fortune to work directly with either Professor Seirul·lo or Professor Frade, as many others from my generation, we were directly or indirectly inspired by their experiences and knowledge. Their works helped in shaping my own multidisciplinary, holistic and complex approach to football.

Various are the examples of successful coaches that are associated with their methodologies, being Pep Guardiola and José Mourinho the most renowned ones... for sure others will follow, especially if can show the same passion, courage and capacity to challenge and implement innovative practices and solutions.

This book, compiling in detail two of my strongest football methodology references, opens the door to further reflections and a better understanding about the Iberian football coaching successes, we've witnessed over the last decades. Congratulations to Javier on putting this quality work together, and especially for giving the opportunity to English readers to access such valuable authors, whose work are published mainly in Portuguese and/or Spanish. Hope you can read it open minded and pick from each one of them new ideas that help developing your coaching processes and successes.

FOREWORD

by Rafael Martín Acero[2]

Seirul·lo: training the footballer for football, from the neuroscientific foundations of complexity

Francisco Seirul·lo is a coach, professor and master with a great transcendence in the transformation of Spanish´s high performance sport. His field experience and academic profile, in teaching and in investigation, has had and still has an undeniable influence in the performance methodology in several sports, promoting a training practice in Spain during the last forty years which has facilitated many of its coaches and sportsmen successes.

The sporting successes of Professor Seirul·lo have verified his proposals scientifically founded on the complexity theories and neuroscience. He has directly participated in singular successes, but it has been the whole of them which has given more visibility to his praxis, turning it into stigmatic for many coaches and scholars. This new approach, both practical and theoretical, has been named by some as Seirul·lo´s thinking or paradigm. Its influence on sport training has been deep and extensive, having worked directly as a sports coach in football, handball, track and field, judo, tennis or motorbiking.

The current book written by Javier Mallo represents a unique opportunity to learn about Professor Seirul·lo´s work, which is a necessary task. There is a web (www.entrenamientodeportivo.org) which collects many of Seirul·lo´s documents. Additionally, the Master´s course organised by F.C. Barcelona´s Foundation and INEFC, also brings together a part of the knowledge on fitness training for team sports built after Seirul·lo. The impact on practice of Seirul·lo cannot be quantifiable. Many of the investigations and doctoral theses have had

---

[2] PhD. Sport Performance Expert. Current Coordinator of the Performance Support Service at R.C. Deportivo de La Coruña (since 1999). Former Dean of the Faculty of Sports Sciences (Universidad La Coruña, 1998-2013) and Sprint Coach of Spain national athletics team (1986-1992).

a greater impact than any standardised academic contribution. As an academic, Seirul·lo has taught subjects in university education as motor control, kinesiology and sports training.

Lalín (2009), fitness coach at R.C. Deportivo de La Coruña (1999-2008), Real Madrid (2008-2013) and Chelsea F.C. (2014-2015), remembers that Professor Seirul·lo had already synthesised how fitness coaches should handle the specialised work for injury prevention and re-adaptation in the 1980s. This complements the observations carried out by Fernández del Olmo (2009), motor control researcher and coach in different elite teams (R. C. Deportivo de La Coruña, Liceo H.C.), about Professor Seirul·lo´s scientific approach to the performance factors of the elite player and the effects that training situations, as systematised causes, produce in the player to achieve a continuous enhancement of his motor behaviour during the competitive game. Seirul·lo was ahead of his time applying what is today known as proprioceptive functional training. His neurophysiological knowledge of the functional units of the human psychomotor system have allowed him, since four decades ago, to develop such a foresighted approach on the current contributions on human movement of neurosciences and complexity sciences.

Seirul·lo has influenced and provided the most suggestive hypotheses and building blocks for team sports training, in particular for football and handball. His contributions on the new physical activity and sports sciences are countless, with many of them having a great influence on real practice, having been very well addressed in this good book by Javier Mallo. Seirul·lo has also had a great influence on the training of numerous coaches. Guardiola, who was coached by Seirul·lo since he was 14 years old and with whom he worked during all his successful management years at Barça, can be cited as an example. In addition, he also worked with Johan Cruyff, Robson, Rexach, Van Gaal, Rijkaard, Villanova and Martino. Regarding handball, he always worked together with Valero Ribera, the world´s most decorated coach in the sport, both at Barça and at the Spanish national team.

Frade: Training the team for the game, from the foundations of the theories of complexity

Other materials, very well collected by Javier Mallo in this book, are based on another very good practice also stigmatised by its success, known as Tactical Periodisation Model. This practice has had a proximal and parallel development to what we have called Seirul·lo´s Cognitive Model of Synergistic Functionality. It should not have just a mere anecdote value the fact that Seirul·lo and Mourinho coincided during five years in FC Barcelona´s coaching staff (under the management of Robson and Van Gaal), at the same time as it is not just anecdotic about Rui Faria´s, Mourinho´s assistant, study placement at FC Barcelona. Additionally, the contemporary cultural and academical proximity of two university professors in Barcelona (Seirul·lo, with responsibility in high competition football training) and Porto (Frade, also with practical training responsibilities) should not remain as another coincidence.

The Tactical Periodisation Model was studied, developed and put in to practical value, among others, by Rui Faria (1999, 2003), especially since his encounter with José Mourinho, more than a decade ago. These specialists, with a deep formation and an extensive experience, have definitively contributed to a new vision of football´s training practice and theory. Most probably, it is also no coincidence that both of them are physical education professionals, confronting a very complex sport as football, which is very difficult to study and to scientifically analyse. This convergence of interests, visions and approaches have a very good reflection in the words of Vítor Frade when he says "my current elite reference coach is José Mourinho´s method and my football´s game model reference is Pep Guardiola´s."

I wish that the author´s efforts to collect the most successful worldwide football tendencies during the last few decades, and with the best foundation and theoretical references in this book, achieves its objectives: That the work of southern European coaches becomes better known for the majority of football coaches.

FOREWORD

by Xavier Tamarit[3]

"Either you believe in it, or you don´t; there is no intermediary position!"

With each passing day I am more and more convinced that Rui Faria (José Mourinho´s assistant coach, currently working at Chelsea F.C.) is absolutely right on this phrase which he used to conclude the foreword of my last book (Tamarit, 2013). Moreover, even in my first book (Tamarit, 2007) I said: *"Tactical Periodisation is something you believe in or you don´t, you are either for it or against it. You cannot say, I believe in it but... Then it is no longer Tactical Periodisation."*

And this has nothing to do with extremisms and radicalisms, but with the loss of Meaning of a Logic that is (il)logical according to the conventional thinking, and which suffers the risk of really being illogical if we do not part with certain conventional dependencies.

Now, the dominance of the question at issue is just as important as the belief. Should this happen, it would be very complicated to accurately differentiate between x and y, as it would be very easy for our subconscious to trick us, based on its deep-rooted understanding which we have been formed from as children and which prevents us from seeing things as they are presented to us, and which takes us to a lack of consistency and to the above-mentioned loss of Meaning.

But be careful: this conventionalism that rules our way of thinking and feeling, both in our consciousness and, even worse, in our subconsciousness, has nothing to do with training with the ball or without the ball, or with training with games or in a more analytical way, or with using more generic or specific drills, or with having a greater or smaller "systemic" thinking...

---

[3] *Degree in Sports Sciences. Author of the books "¿Qué es la "Periodización Táctica?" (What is Tactical Periodisation?) and "Periodización Táctica v Periodización Táctica" (Tactical Periodisation v Tactical Periodisation). Former Assistant Coach at Valencia CF (Spain) and Estudiantes de la Plata (Argentina).*

There are times in which at first sight may seem, when observing some training units, that training is following this methodology. This happens when training is carried out in a unique training unit per day, in most of the cases with the presence of the ball, even including specific situations related to the Game Model, on some days based on more individual or sectorial game features while on other days based on more collective elements... But Tactical Periodisation is much more, or less, than all of this. It is an understanding form different to the conventional way: understanding the Human being and its functioning, understanding the organism and its adaptability, understanding the playing and its production... And it is not only diverse in its way of understanding but also in its way of operationalising and proceeding! To achieve this it is necessary to show respect for some Methodological Principles (Principle of Propensities, Principle of Complex Progression and Principle of Horizontal Alternation in specificity) which, being correctly understood and taken to the field, enable that Logic.

And it is not easy to divest from the thinking in which we have been formed. For example, and knowing it is just one more drop in a full glass, there are many times in which I have regretted having written about the coffee with milk strategy. I have the sensation of having played right into the hands a perfect excuse for the conscious, in the case of many, and/or the subconscious, in the case of few, preventing myself from loosing the hand from the logic with which we have learned to walk and without which we are threatened to fall in the ground. The coffee and milk strategy must only be used only in the context and situations which require it, and always being related to disappear as soon as possible. In addition, it requires a great control and knowledge on what we are doing so it does not generate incoherence with the process matrix, that is, with the Tactical Periodisation Logic.

Ultimately, carried away by this way of thinking which has been imposed on us and which confuses us because of our incomplete proficiency of the things, we do something, intentionally or not, which in its form looks like Tactical Periodisation but in its essence it is incoherent with its Logic. We are neither "here" nor "there" and we generate a process with a lack of harmony which usually takes us to unwanted individual and/or collective performances, blaming Tactical Periodisation for them... but which Tactical Periodisation are we talking about? The one created by Vítor Frade[4] or our own undermined and incoherent version?

This common incongruousness which is concomitant to the process does not allow Specificity, which leads to adaptability, to manifest, and vice-versa, in a continuos loop. Specificity a *sine qua non* condition of this methodology and, thus, without it Tactical Periodisation is no longer Tactical Periodisation. This is why there is no intermediary position, either by belief or by lack of insight.

The author of this book, through the way of his writing, sparks the interest of readers to avoid becoming isolated or marking time in the previously acquired knowledge. Thus, the constant search and the need to reflect and question, even our own reflections, should continuously guide our development.

I decided to write this foreword without personally knowing Javier and without having read the book in its entirety. I did it because of the daring, solidarity and dedication that emanates from it. Daring to try to show that there are new horizons in the insight and understanding of football, of the game and its training, confronting all the institutionalised knowledge that this involves. Solidarity for sharing the knowledge which was so hard for him to acquire, and the experiences which underpins it, this being the only way to keep evolving and improving as a society, in any of its dimensions, football in this case. And dedication for what writing and editing a book of this magnitude implies, moreover in a language other than his native tongue.

This book is a good starting point, I reiterate, to question certain established "truths" and, in the case of doubting, encourages to further research and the necessity, which should be implicit, to immerse in the deep, without staying in the comfortable surface which does not allow one to appreciate the abyssal zone[5] of the things.

---

[4] *Vítor Frade is the creator of Tactical Periodisation and its maximum referent.*
[5] *Abyssal zone: Is one of the levels in which the ocean is divided into according to its depth, which is between 2000 and 6000 meters. It represents, approximately, 70% of the oceans. This zone is almost unknown for human beings because of the existent conditions as a lack of sunlight and an elevated hydrostatic pressure. As an example, we know more about Mars than about this zone.*

INTRODUCTION

"Insanity: doing the same thing over and over again and expecting different results"

Albert Eisntein

In the year 1994 United States of America hosted the 15th edition of the FIFA World Cup. Many specialists dared to predict that this country was going to dominate football in the near future due to their vast population, economic power and sporting structure. Despite having more than 300 million inhabitants, the highest gross domestic product in the world (according to the International Monetary Fund) and winning the greatest number of Olympic medals in London 2012, their national football team has only reached the World Cup semi-finals back in 1930. In their latest participations —South Africa 2010 and Brazil 2014— USA reached the round of 16.

On the other hand, Uruguay´s population is below 3.5 million, holds the 77th position in the gross domestic product world ranking (year 2012) and did not get a single medal in the 2012 Olympic Games. However, they finished in third position in the 2010 World Cup held in South Africa, augmenting their successful record after being World Cup winners in 1930 and 1950 and finishing third in the 1954 and 1970 editions. Additionally, they lost to France in the penalty shoot-out in the final game of the last Under 20 World Championship Turkey 2013.

If we attend to traditional thinking, it is difficult to find an explanation to these facts. Attending to a World Cup requires a squad formed by 23 footballers and, for instance, it would be much easier to produce a world class athlete in an individual sport rather than completing a football team. Nevertheless, Uruguay, with almost 1% of USA´s population and 0.3% of its gross domestic product, has been able to produce better footballers during the last few years. Reinforcing this idea, two players from Uruguay, Edinson Cavani and Luis Suarez, figured in the 23-man shortlist for the 2013 FIFA Ballon d´Or which was compiled by the FIFA Football Committee and a group of experts from France Football, with none of the players born in the USA were in this final list.

Using similar reasoning strategies, pseudo-football experts also foresighted great success for African national teams after their dominance in the youth tournaments. During the last 25 years (between 1988 and 2013), African countries have reached ten semi-final presences at the Under-17 level and another ten at the Under-20 level. Ghana (two time winners and six time runners-up in the Under-17 and Under-20 age groups combined) and Nigeria (three titles and four-time finalist) have been the most successful nations, probably due to their physical superiority. However, despite these 20 appearances in the rounds of last four, an African national team has never reached the semi-finals of the World Cup at the senior level yet, leaving Cameroon (1994), Senegal (2002) and Ghana (2010) as the best placed teams, which, in all cases, was the quarter-finals. If it is not about population, money, sporting resources or physicality, what is happening here? Why are people unable to produce top-class footballers and winning teams? Are the experts missing the critical ingredients of the magic potion?

During my years as a Professor at the Faculty of Physical Activity and Sport Sciences of the Technical University of Madrid, I lectured on the subject "Football." To establish a coherent starting line I tried to adapt the teaching contents to the course objectives, which were very similar to those necessary to obtain the UEFA coaching licenses. Nevertheless, I soon became aware of some basic fundamental differences between the tactical principles I had to academically follow and those which I had experienced in my previous professional coaching roles.

Under these constraints I had to reverse the direction of the approach and, instead of explaining tactical principles to be used in the game (as covers, pressing, support, overloading and so on), I studied the game and then looked for principles to explain what had happened. That is, I tried to diagnose teams and footballers performances in competition, searching for qualitative elements that should have requested deeper attention during the training process. Hence, the most successful teams of the moment were selected for analysis to identify the main features of their Playing Models and to try to detect the Game Principles which characterised each moment of the game. Complementarily and to take a broader view, the second half of the task was to investigate the training methodology of top-class teams, in order to understand the practical requirements which were needed to develop a particular Playing Model. Two main references were inexcusable to mention in all football debates at this stage: FC Barcelona and José Mourinho. As a personal research aim, I dedicated my time to get as much information as possible from these two playing and training philosophies, reading, traveling, watching training sessions and talking to people who were familiar with both ideas.

FC Barcelona represents a traditional excellent taste for offensive football, inherited from the management times of Johan Cruyff. Frank Rijkaard and, especially, Pep Guardiola took the club to the greatest standard with a team basically formed with home-grown talents, which unanimously won the whole world´s applause with its style of play. In June 2014, former FC Barcelona player Luis Enrique was appointed as the new First Team manager trying to keep alive the uniqueness of the Club´s interpretation of football. Looking deeper into the training methodology roots, the figure of Paco Seirul·lo appears to be a common link between the successive development phases of the last few decades.

The ability of José Mourinho —alongside with his inseparable ideological mate Rui Faria— to win titles in different countries and his enthralling personality are qualities that almost every coach wants for himself. Many coaches have tried to replicate Mourinho´s characteristics and pose; but sooner rather than later have failed to reach success, having forgotten to include one of the major ingredients of his receipt: the training methodology. His biographical references from Benfica, Uniao de Leiria, Porto, Chelsea, Inter and Real Madrid, led me to an encounter with one crucial topic: Tactical Periodisation, a concept developed in detail by Vítor Frade at the University of Porto (Portugal).

Even though many people will consider FC Barcelona and José Mourinho´s training philosophies being antagonistic, there are plenty of meeting points between them. Probably, the most important of them is the rupture with the traditional approach to football training, where the body was conceived as a machine and was studied relying on measurable disciplines as physiology, biomechanics, physics or anatomy. The reality of football is far more complicated that this simplistic approach and recalls the necessity of including new sciences in the equation. Psychology, cognitivism, anthropology, structuralism, cybernetics, systems theory, chaos theory, neuroscience, fractal geometry or ecology also need to be addressed to develop an integral representation of the football player, where body and mind are always inter-related and cannot be considered in isolation. Therefore, complexity sciences provide the foundations for a new qualitative paradigm to study football and its training process, away from the traditional convention which has been followed during many years. Thus, we need to overpass the "streetlight effect" where people only look for whatever they are searching by looking where it is easiest, as the following parable tells (Freedman, 2010, after Kaplan, 1964):

> *A policeman sees a drunk man searching for something under a streetlight and asks what the drunk has lost. He says he lost his keys and they both look under the streetlight together. After a few minutes the policeman asks if he is sure he lost them there, and the drunk replies, no, and that he lost them in the park. The policeman asks why he is searching here, and the drunk replies, 'This is where the light is.'*

Professor Seirul·lo (from Barcelona, developing the concept of Structured Training) and Professor Frade (from Porto, Tactical Periodisation) have provided a valuable support to all of us who think that there is another way to do things in football. Unfortunately, most of their research has been published in Spanish and Portuguese, respectively, which represents a linguistic barrier that has limited the divulgation of their knowledge. This is one of the main reasons for this book, which tries to bring together as much information as possible from some of the original sources available in the literature. The fundamental ideas have been gathered and the basic concepts translated, to introduce coaches to this exciting way to understand football training. Nevertheless, it will always represent an incomplete trip so it is highly recommended to read directly from the main experts (Paco Seirul·lo, Vítor Frade, Albert Roca, Guillerme Oliveira, Xavier Tamarit, Marisa Silva, Miguel Tavares or Bruno Oliveira and colleagues, etc.) to have a wider and more precise perspective of the research question and to avoid translation misunderstandings. Of special interest is the recent book about Tactical Periodisation written by Xavier Tamarit, who brilliantly unites Vítor Frade´s direct testimonies. In addition,

Introduction

quotations from Seirul·lo, Frade and Mourinho will be provided in the text to help the reader understand the peculiarities of each training methodology.

Finally, and before you start reading the book, I have one suggestion: Erase your mind, clean your previous football thoughts and forget everything you have learned about training so far. This is not as easy as it seems and even Albert Einstein anticipated this by saying, "What a sad era when it is easier to smash an atom than a prejudice." Once you have a clean mind, try to understand the basic concepts of Structured Training and Tactical Periodisation and, when you finish the book, go back to your reality. Then, you will probably have additional resources and tools which you might employ in the training of your team. It is not about which methodology is better than the other one or which one will make your team win more matches. It is about understanding the person and the game, setting the foundations to take footballers and teams to a superior optimised level.

©Víctor Salgado/F.C.Barcelona

PART I

THE NEED FOR A PARADIGM SHIFT IN SCIENCE AND FOOTBALL

"I think the next century will be the century of complexity"

Stephen Hawking

I.1 TRADITIONAL APPROACH TO FOOTBALL TRAINING

I.1.1 Foundations of sports training

Training organisation is a very popular phenomenon in modern sport but, if we go back to the Ancient Greek and Roman eras many centuries ago, we realise that things have not changed much during the years. Hegedüs (1988) explains how athletes were prepared to take part in the preterit Olympic Games during a ten month long preparation period, which concluded with a one month training camp. This training period was further divided into shorter —four days— cycles called *tetras* which were consecutively repeated until the start of the competition. The daily routine of these primitive athletes mainly consisted of sleeping, training, nutrition and having philosophical debates which, except for the last element, is a very similar pattern to the principles shared by present-day coaches. The book "Gymnasticus", written by Philostratus, is probably one of the first references to this year long training organisation, at the same time describing the specific physical profile needed to take part in each type of athletic discipline (Konig, 2009). Galen (129-210 AD) is another representative thinker from this period and in the essay "Preservation of Health" presented a detailed categorisation of training exercises and their sequencing during the season (Issurin, 2010).

It was not until the re-establishment of the Olympic Games in the last years of the nineteenth century when interest in training methodology was again documented. Pikhala published a book in 1930 containing statements that have reached our days: work and recovery have to be alternated during the season, generic training must precede specific training and the increase of intensity should be related to a decrease in the training volume (Hegedüs, 1988). Additionally, the annual plan was divided into four stages: preparation, spring, summer and recovery (autumn), with competitions concentrated in the two central periods.

There are plenty of references from different authors such as Murphy (1913), Kotov (1917), Gorinewsky (1922), Birsin (1925), Vsorov (1938), Grantyn (1939), Dyson (1946) or Letunov (1950) who investigated on training organisation during the first half of the twentieth century (Seirul·lo, 1987a; Siff & Verkhoshansky, 2000). After the success of Russian athletes during the 1950s, Matveiev (1964) was probably the first author to explain the general rules used by these athletes to organise the training loads during the season. Matveiev became the most recognised figure from these years setting the foundations for periodisation in sport and influenced many other posterior classic publications such as Ozolin (1970), Harre (1973), Dick (1980), Bompa (1984) or Platonov (1988). Matveiev´s design of the season commenced with a preparation period (subdivided into a generic and a special phase), which was followed by a competition period and concluded with a transition period between seasons (Matveiev, 1977, 1982, 1985).

This periodisation model was widely accepted by coaches and applied in the majority of sports. However, during the last decades different authors have questioned this universal approach to training as it does not fulfil the peculiarities of all sport disciplines and elite practitioners. Matveiev´s traditional design was focused on taking part in one main competition during the season (two to three competitions per year at the most) and differentiated between generic and specific preparation, with oscillations in the volume and intensity curves. Issurin (2008, 2012) summarised some of the drawbacks of this conventional approach to periodisation: prolonged workloads, negative interaction of some of these loads, not enough training stimulus for elite athletes, etc. These limitations did not allow sportsmen to reach their maximum potential in many competitions during the season. Thus, the need for multi-peak performances required reductions in the overall training volume and the implementation of more specialised training workloads, which led to the development of block periodisation models as an alternative season design (Bondarchuk, 1988; Verkhoshansky, 1990).

Coaches have tried to find specific planning models that best suit their particular disciplines and, for instance, concepts as reverse periodisation have been recently introduced in individual sports as a variation in the way to organise the training loads within the season (King, 2000). Reverse periodisation (very briefly explained, from anaerobic to aerobic) has become popular during the last years in endurance sports as athletes begin the season developing foundations of speed, power and specific endurance, which allows taking part in competitions from an early stage of the season. This represents an antagonistic approach to traditional periodisation (from aerobic to anaerobic) where athletes devote the initial part of the season to basic capacities, with the consequent impossibility to successfully perform in competitions during this build up period. However, the real effect of these alternative periodisation models on team sports (block, reverse, etc.), which have proven successful in certain individual sports, still remains unclear.

Due to the lack of complementary relevant information, many coaches continue to apply generic principles of individual sports training to team sports, even though there are scarce similarities between them. Furthermore, team sports that share epistemological roots as American football and European football (soccer) present such a different playing dynamic that it seems questionable that they could share a common training philosophy. Playing the ball with the feet is an obvious characteristic which sets critical differences with any other sport and determines a communication matrix that cannot be replicated under any other environment. This peculiar configuration of its internal logic (Parlebas, 2001) gives football a special aesthetic and uncertainty, representing a worldwide attraction as a superb spectacle and a new direction into which one can investigate about its training organisation.

I.1.2 The influence of Classical Thinking on the theory and practice of sports training

Martín Acero & Vittori (1997, in Martín Acero & Lago, 2005a) believe that the methodology of sporting performance should aim to examine the scientific and pedagogic foundations that lead from the possibilities of performance to their availability in competition. The conceptual basis for the development of training methods for individual sports such as swimming, athletics or cycling was justified after the identification of the components of the competition workload in each discipline. The information extracted from the analysis of competition was integrated into performance models (Bompa, 1984). A model is an "imitation or simulation of reality, built after specific elements of the phenomenon which is observed and investigated" (Navarro, 1997).

The development of a model is a process than can take several years, as it requires eliminating wrong components and introducing new ones. The first steps to design a model are the contemplation phase, where the coach or researcher observes and analyses the sport, and the inference phase, where the elements that must be retained are selected and those irrelevant rejected. Later, the quantitative and qualitative elements are introduced and refined, and the model is tested under training and competition situations until consolidating its final version (Bompa, 1984). In relation with this matter, González Badillo (2002) affirms:

> *The analysis model has the aim of selecting, describing and interpreting (explaining) the processes and characteristics of the studied sporting activity; verifying the theoretical assumptions and the data admitted as valid in relation to the general theory of sporting performance and of each particular speciality; and predicting, after the information provided by the model, the occurrence of certain processes and results.*

Hay & Reid´s (1982) model has been widely employed to explain a hierarchy and relationship between the factors that might affect sport performance. These authors described the creation of a model by systematically examining the performance of a skill, showing the connections between a particular result and the elements which influenced it. The use of this kind of block diagrams can help to determine which contributory factors should be improved to enhance overall performance.

Following the influence of authors as Matveiev (1977), Bompa (1984) or Platonov (1988), sporting performance was divided into separate areas: fitness, technique, tactics or psychology. Each area was further subdivided according to the key performance indicators, so specific training methods were developed to improve each element on isolation and maximise the outcome in the sport. This generic approach shows a great reminiscence from Classical Thinking and follows the second maxim from Descartes´ "Discourse on the Method": fragmenting a problem into as many simple and separated elements as possible.

Pragmatic thinking strategies have been the foundation for the development of science (Balagué & Torrents, 2011) and, since the times of Galileo (sixteenth-seventeenth century), there has been an obsession with measuring and quantifying all kind of phenomena (Capra, 1996). Newton´s mathematical reasoning and Laplace´s studies supported Descartes´ dissertations and influenced an atomistic interpretation of nature, which could be explained in the same way as the working of a perfect machine, built with smaller pieces without relationships between them. Hence, the whole could be divided into separate parts and everything in the world could be predicted and explained with exact mathematical laws. Once the observer has the capacity to abstract himself from the environment, he can independently study the parts and, from them, understand the whole (Balagué & Torrents, 2011).

This conceptual framework resulted in ancestral dialogical confrontations: body versus mind, science versus philosophy, subject versus object, theory *versus* practice, and so on. Surprisingly, it still has an enormous influence in our days, as we are living in a society extremely affected by compartmentalisation and reductionism (Morin, 2000). The method of analytical thinking, created by Descartes, can be summarised in the following three steps (Monzó, 2006): i) dividing a complex phenomenon into smaller pieces, ii) trying to understand the behaviour of each part on its own, and iii) understanding the properties of the whole from the properties of the different parts.

The fragmentation of knowledge into independent disciplines encourages people to be analytical, to reduce things from complex to simple, instead of building a global concept of the world. By doing so, science builds its object away from its environment, putting it into non-complex experimental situations (Morin, 1994). Sport science faculties maintain reminiscences from the Cartesian mechanism and present a diversity of knowledge areas such as physiology, biomechanics, anthropology, psychology, sociology, motor control or theory and practice of training in an attempt to examine human movement from as many different perspectives as possible. However, in many cases, the process has taken the opposite direction to that desired, isolating knowledge instead of helping to understand human complexity.

The study of the sportsman has traditionally fallen into this deterministic view of nature. Performance components were identified, isolated and disintegrated into simpler elements. Once done, it was intended that by modifying one variable at a time generic laws could be elaborated, in order to predict the behaviour of the system under different conditions (Martín Acero & Lago, 2005a). Conceiving the human being in this way mutilates his peculiar personal characteristics, as he is considered like a machine that can be externally programmed to linearly respond to the applied stimulus, with no interaction with the environment. Product is favoured over process and mathematical algorithms are searched to explain cause-effect relationships between its different parts and the functioning of the whole.

Competition analysis in collective sports has habitually followed this kind of mechanistic procedures and team performance has been examined studying the individual performances of the players who were part of the squad. Therefore, all the initial investigations were carried out through the lens of individual sports, fragmenting the performance factors to be able to apply the principles which had been shown effective for athletes in certain disciplines (Lago, 2002). This way to proceed ignored the complex range of interactions which can be found between the members of a team. Moreover, the final performance was represented as a sum of factors which were independently treated during the training process, without a direct relationship with the reality of the game (Hernández Moreno, 2001; Mombaerts, 1998).

Football has not been immune to this factorial tendency and both the player and the game have been uncoupled to be studied away from their specific context. This thinking strategy has led to the division of the player into separated dimensions (physical, technical, tactical and mental/psychological) or disjoining the moments of the game (attack, defence, attack-defence transition and defence-attack transition). This kind of analysis allows deeper levels of study, as the physical capacities can be classified into strength, endurance or speed, and even be further subdivided into explosive, elastic, reactive strength, and so on.

Most of the initial research in football was carried out under the influence of behaviouristic psychology and the interest of the studies was placed on what the player was able to do, that is, the observed conduct. Ekblom (1986) was one of the first authors to report a physiological performance model in football, taking into consideration information from the temporal characteristics and physical requirements of the game, and the physiological profile of the footballers. Similarly, Bangsbo (1994) determined the demands of football by taking relevant observations during match-play, obtaining physiological measurements during training and competition, and examining the physical capacity of elite players.

The integration of information from competition with that from successful footballers has been the most extended research approach to our days. Recent studies have concluded that a top-class professional player covers between 10 and 12 km during a competitive match, with distance covered at high-intensities (>14 km/h) amounting for around 20-25% of total match distance (Bradley *et al.*, 2009; Dellal *et al.*, 2011; Rampinini *et al.*, 2007). These physical demands can be influenced by a variety of factors such as the playing position, standard of competition, percentage of ball possession, moment of the season, training status, etc. (Bloomfield *et al.*, 2007; Di Salvo *et al.*, 2007; Gregson *et al.*, 2010; Mohr *et al.*, 2003). The average cardiac values that a football match demands on a player represent around 85% of the individual maximal heart rate (Stolen *et al.*, 2005). Regarding the anthropometric profile of top-class players, mean stature is around 1.80-1.85 m, with 75-80 kg of body mass. Other physical capacities which have been examined in this population of footballers reveal the following average characteristics: VO_2max values ranging between 60-65 ml/kg/min, anaerobic threshold running speed at 14 km/h, countermovement jumping height of 50 cm, sprinting 20 m in less than 3 s and half squatting strength of 200 kg (Hoff, 2005; Stolen *et al.*, 2005). Many of the physical capacities examined in these kinds of studies underestimate the load taking capacity of the muscle, as physical performance is not so much about distance covered or heart rate values but about the ability to repeatedly accelerate and decelerate during the game.

The great majority of the investigations published so far refer to conditional or bio-energetic requirements, which have favoured the development of physical performance models for footballers. Nowadays, elite clubs have their own semi-automatic image recognition systems (Prozone, Amisco, etc.) to track their players during competition and calculate individual physical parameters on a match-by-match frequency. Data obtained when using these procedures include the total distance covered, high intensity running, number of sprints or distance covered by sprinting, which can be expressed in relation to match intervals or to other variables as if the team is in or out of ball possession. These parameters are used to establish individual baselines and allow comparisons with teammates and opponents. In addition, technical performance data from an individual and collective point of view (such as number of passes, passing accuracy, key passes, goals, shots on goal, total number of shots, assistances, crosses, tackles, clearances, interceptions, blocks or duels) are also available in the post-match analysis. The collection of all this information makes the determination of specific physical and technical performance models for each particular player or team possible.

Complementing the analysis of competition, monitoring and quantifying training load represents another key issue in sport (Mújika, 2013) and has become an essential competency for sport scientists and fitness coaches. The need for certainties has enhanced the importance of collecting as much measurable data as possible from training sessions: distances covered, heart rates, number of jumps, passes, duels, rates of perceived exertion, blood samples, etc. A great number of technologies have proliferated during the last few years to help this process with the aim of accurately evaluating performance during training, trying to have an objective control of the situation.

Many coaches have found comfort under this mechanistic conception of modern football as, to a certain extent, "It seems that what cannot be quantified does not exist" (Lillo, in Cano, 2009). The information provided by match analysis tools or fitness tests allows decomposing the performance of the footballers into different areas, searching for critical indicators, and once those relevant variables are identified, training is oriented on improving them in isolation. That is, individual values are compared to the reference performance models, determining the starting position of the player and identifying the final parameters to be achieved, so the coach just needs to follow previously validated training programs to take the footballer through a closed pathway. Therefore, if a player shows a decrement in high-intensity running in the last stages of a match, a conditioning coach would be in charge of improving his aerobic fitness. Complementarily, if a player performs poorly in a repeated sprint ability test, training should be focused on the anaerobic metabolism. Furthermore, if a footballer shows a bad accuracy percentage in short-distance passing, then the skills coach would work on his passing abilities during the following week.

The training tasks and methods used to take the footballer through this closed process are known as "exercises progressions" or "pedagogic progressions" (Seirul·lo, 1999). Every player who follows the same sequence should reach an identical ending stage. This gives the coach an essential role in the process: he is in charge of transmitting the information to the sportsman through a one-direction communication channel. The footballer learns by the repetition of exercises which have been previously identified and accepted as a generic pathway for all kind of players. The exercises sequencing and progression are based on the previous experiences of the coach, feeding the false assumption that there are no other possible alternatives (Balagué & Torrents, 2011).

Under this conventional conception of the training process, the coach keeps his field of authority as he commands the growth of the player. The capacity to have an absolute control of the situation is the desire of many coaches, and in being able to do so, it is easier to have disciplined pupils rather than people who think of alternatives. This linear intervention helps the development of robotic footballers who need the constant external feedback from the coach to act during the match. The coach tends to narrow the freedom of the player with statements as, "When you see the fullback driving the ball, go to press him." These kinds of automatisms are learned by footballers, underestimating the variability of the situations which can happen during the game. In this scenario, even top-class coaches such as Wanderley Luxemburgo defended the benefits of players using headphones during the game to listen to the instructions of the coach (Borasteros, 2005).

Coaches who share this philosophy would be happy to attend to the RoboCup, where teams of robots play against each other. The objective of these programmers is to beat a human World Cup winning team with a team formed by autonomous robots, under the official FIFA rules, before the year 2050 (Kitano & Asada, 2002). Fortunately, players as Messi, Ibrahimovic, Pirlo, Luis Suárez, Ribéry, Agüero, Silva, Iniesta or Xavi, who have not followed the standardised education pattern and their physical profile is different to that suggested by the so called experts, are the most determining in contemporary football, as they are able to produce unpredictable behaviours. Jorge Valdano —World Cup winner as a player and a former Real Madrid manager— sheds light to this topic by saying (in Suárez, 2012):

> *At present, Messi does everything faster and better than any other. He wins games on his own, and many games. Even if his creative patterns are discovered, there is no way to stop him. The only way is in a pack or outside the rules. Agüero and Tévez take you to the primitive game, with the aspect of being fearless. Tévez once told that he suffered a shooting at his door step and everybody threw themselves to the ground. How can you talk about scenic fear to someone who has had bullets crossing over him? When so many people are pretending to reduce the risks of football, the appearance of these kinds of figures who laugh about all formulas is very healthy. They are not aware of any formula and, on the other hand, they solve all of them.*

Most of the actual formal teaching and learning systems are structured under the same kind of principles, which restrict the development and demonstration of talent and creativity. Instead, society searches for meek individuals who do not compromise the messages from the governing authority, building people without discordant thoughts. Football training programs have taken steps in the same direction, which will probably lead to homogenise the level of the players around the world, proliferating middle-class industrialised footballers. That is, all players are tarred with the same brush: positional specialised, well-developed physically and with a correct use of all the basic technical skills. Not surprisingly, Valdano (in Cano, 2009) claims "if we are only building obedient players we cannot criticise that we are lacking of leaders."

Traditional training programs rely on the logical and rational part of the brain (the left hemisphere), whereas the right side (in charge of emotions and creativity) receives little attention. The stimulation of both hemispheres of the brain has been proved to enhance the acquisition of multiple cognitive and motor skills and, therefore, should be prevalent during football training. During the subsequent years, neuroscience studies will help to increase our knowledge about how our brain learns and the neuronal changes during this process. The design and implementation of variable tasks during the training strategy of the coach will probably stimulate the plasticity of the brain and the creation of new synapses in the nervous system of the players. This seems essential as "football is born in the brain, not in the body" (Sacchi, in Wilson, 2013). These tasks should promote interactions between the footballers, as intelligence is developed when people collaborate and cooperate with other people to solve problems (Punset, 2007). Additionally, the coach needs to be aware of how to manage emotions during the training and learning process.

Football clubs currently operate as big business companies, having incorporated attractive organisation charts. People in the highest positions of the club hierarchy hold an economic background and are more familiar with numeric data, graphs and audiovisual presentations than with parameters which try to explain the complexity of the game. This is why the quantification and modelling of team performance through objective data represents an irresistible temptation to people who live around the sport but do not really understand it.

This technological conception of football has justified the proliferation of specialists for the differentiated interpretation and treatment of each performance component. In this sense, modern clubs are proud to be considered as sophisticated Formula-1 teams, where engineers are in charge of the correct functioning of each of the pieces the car. Under this theoretical paradigm, a perfect assembly of the parts would allow achieving a superior whole and a complete knowledge of the object of study. This has resulted in the hyper-specialisation of realities, eliminating all sources that can compromise absolute certainties (Morin, 1994), as we prefer conceiving reality as a simple model that we can understand (Krishna, 2004, in Cano, 2009).

Coherent as this theoretical approach might seem, there are several drawbacks that compromise the universal acceptance of this operation strategy and, when taken into practice, important problems arise, principally due to the lack of a common language: football (Verheijen, 2013). Each of the experts can be a world-class eminency in his discipline but lacks insight from the essential element which contextualises the situation. Therefore, the gurus who take adjacent roles to the management staff test and verify their own hypotheses under a partial reconstruction of reality, away from competition constraints, and barricade themselves in their own particular knowledge. By doing so, theories are developed away from real game circumstances (Cano, 2009), without respecting the interaction between the sub-systems of the players and the environment (Araújo et al., 2006). O´Connor & McDermott (1997) metaphorically alert about this procedure by arguing that nobody would take apart a piano to look for its sound. As so much data can be collected during a match, a numerical excuse to justify defeat can always be found by each specialist.

To illustrate this operating strategy and its limitations we can use a practical example. A top-class team carries out fitness tests at the end of the preparation period and a player shows a slow time in a speed (20 m) test. After analysing all the scores, the management staff determines that the player needs special sprint training to improve his running speed, so the club hires the best sprint coach in the country, in charge of top-class athletes. Having carried out specific sprint training drills for two months, the player repeats the test improving his previous score by 0.05 s. The staff members get together and congratulate each other for their job. However, even though the player is faster in 20 m linear running many questions can arise: Is the running time improvement greater than the error of the measuring tool? Did the player sprint at his fastest speed in both occasions? Did the sprint training contents and time exposure interfere with team training? And most importantly, is the player faster in a football specific context? This could represent a typical situation in a football team whose working strategy follows a reductionist and deterministic approach. However, in these cases "when results do not happen as expected, *ad hoc* explanations are employed" (Balagué & Torrents, 2011). Going back to the previous example, if after the sprint training intervention the player is not able to show speed improvements under match-play situations, one *ad hoc* explanation by the sprint coach could be that the manager is not playing him in the right position.

It is not surprising to find coaches who have always been working on the field and, in a few seconds and with no other additional tool apart from their experienced senses, are able to identify the key variables to understand a player, a team or a match. However, as it stands now, it appears that some managers do not really understand the game and are unable to extract relevant information from competition. Thus, these kinds of coaches need to surround themselves by consultants who produce quantitative data, which provides them with a greater confidence on what they are doing. For this reason, these coaches search for the application of universal tests to avoid the embarrassment of not being capable of reading the competition, justifying their arguments on statistical parameters which provide a segmented view of the confrontation. Balagué & Torrents (2011) believe, "When measuring, more information than that obtained is lost, independently of employing a rigorous and well-designed protocol." Hence, no matter how much data we collect, it would only give us a false sensation of control, numbing our reflective capacity (Cano, 2009).

Similarly, this tendency can also be observed during training sessions, where some managers delegate most of the training time to other coaches, entertaining players with gym, runs or technical drills, while the head coach is only in charge of the final game at the end of the session, forgetting about the training essence: putting the players to work together to achieve a tactical organisation.

Despite the abundant descriptive data which is currently provided to football coaches, it is essential to increase the quality of the information extracted from competition and training. The intentional activity that players internally process during the game does not necessarily relate to the motor output which is observed and measured by an external observer (Martín Acero & Lago, 2005a). Spanish manager Juanma Lillo (in Cano, 2009) cleverly summarises "intelligence resides in knowing how to live with this certainty, rather than building certainties which make us believe that uncertainty does not exist." Thus, examining the critical (tactical) relationships between teammates and opponents under the competition scenario should be the best tool to asses a player or a team.

I.1.3 New directions to study team sports

As it was discussed in the previous section, the classical approach to the training of team sports has been based on considering the sportsman as a machine, fragmenting his performance components and training these factors in isolation using linear methods, searching for a summation effect at the end of the process.

The influence of behaviouristic psychology is notorious in this traditional conception of training; every response is preceded by a stimulus, without paying importance to the internal occurrences in the person. Thus, under this prism, all the sportsmen who follow the same training program would reach the same ending point. These performance models are developed upon the knowledge of coaches who, based on their individual experiences, believe that their model is the best solution for a particular sport (Seirul·lo, 1999).

Interestingly, we can find plenty of examples of top-class athletes who have escaped from standardised models and their success has eventually modified the universally accepted training postulates. Thus, those coaches who thought that there were no other possible alternatives to their models had to give way to new performance directions. One of the best examples to illustrate this idea was the case of Richard "Dick" Fosbury, who revolutionised the high jump event with his back first technique, later known as the "Fosbury Flop." Despite the sceptical initial reactions of track and field coaches, his jumping technique was adopted by all high jumpers after winning the gold medal in the 1968 Mexico City Olympic Games.

This personal solution to a given situation helps to reinforce the importance of respecting what happens inside the person when he is carrying out any kind of activity, which was the foundation for the development of cognitive theories. Alongside with information processing theories, the application of cybernetics (developed by Wiener in 1948) had a great impact to understand how motor information was coded and processed (Schmidt, 1982). Berstein, between 1930 and 1940, anticipated many of the cybernetic principles and applied them to the learning of motor skills, although his studies were only translated from Russian to English in 1967 (Berstein, 1967). Under this model, the sportsman develops and programs an action project based on his experiences, using intrinsic and extrinsic feedback to adjust his performance (Ruiz Pérez, 1994). Additionally, the environment plays a critical role during the learning processes and cannot be conceived as an independent element.

For these reasons, not all the people react in the same mode to a certain training system or adapt to a universal performance model. This is because every sportsman is influenced by how he processes the information and what happens inside him once he analyses the environment, elaborating his particular way to understand the situation (Seirul·lo, 1999). Thus, Martín Acero et al. (2013) believe that the informational internal load (neurophysiological, perceptive and emotional) is much more important than the external and physiological internal load when examining team sports.

As the traditional approach to training does not seem to fulfil the specific characteristics of team sports, during the last few decades different authors have been working on developing a special theory and practice of training or, more specifically, a general theory of the sporting games (Martín Acero & Lago, 2005a). Being a novel research area, its scientific foundation is still incipient, which makes many people doubt between staying in their comfort zone protected by the traditional theoretical ideas or, alternatively, moving into an unknown land guided by their intuition or experience (Balagué & Torrents, 2011).

Team sports apply a different knowledge field as compared to individual sports and, therefore, extrapolating the models which have been proved successful in individual sports underestimates their different nature (Álvaro, 2002). While individual sports are based habitually on closed abilities carried out in a relatively stable environment, team sports are open abilities (Knapp, 1977, in Gregháigne, 2001), in an unstable environment and with teammates with whom establishing cooperation relationships and opponents that directly interfere in the outcome. In addition to these characteristics Álvaro (2002) adds the necessity of developing discontinue, adaptive and complex conducts in the space and temporal limits dictated by the laws of the sport. Each situation, each game and each competition represents a different narration with similar characteristic elements (Martín Acero & Lago, 2005a).

The book *"El Acto Táctico en Juego"* (The Tactical Act in Play), written by F. Mahlo in 1969, was probably one of the earliest references of a different perspective to interpret collective sports, underlining the necessity of understanding what happens inside the person during the decision making process. In this way, Mahlo introduced a differential component in sports training: the thinking of the sportsman, that is, his implication in solving intrinsic game problems. Given these circumstances, the playing action involves the study of the player while he is playing, forgetting the previous intention of studying the player in isolation.

In the 1970s and 1980s specific models to examine team sports were developed. For instance, the phases of the game model developed by Bayer (1986) — also called functional model in Álvaro *et al.* (1995) — studied the sport in relation to the team in possession of the ball, which defines if a team is in an attacking or defensive phase and, consequently, the roles of the players. The contributions of authors such as Hagedorn (1972), Morino (1985), Godik & Popov (1993) or Bauer (1994) (all of them in Martín Acero & Lago, 2005a) aided to examine the efficiency of the actions of the players at individual, group and team scales. These levels of configuration are extremely important to diagnose team performance and the final competition result and are classified by Martín Acero & Lago (2005a) into the following scales:

- **Micro-structure**: Player individual efficiency in elemental duels (1v1 situations).
- **Meso-structure:** Group efficiency in partial duels (2v2, 3v3 situations).
- **Macro-structure:** Team efficiency in total duels (11v11 situations).

Parlebas presented in 1988 a perspective to study sports focused on the sportsman and the reason for his actions during the game. In his attempt to rationalise motor activities he defined a new knowledge area: praxiology. Accordingly, the objects of study of this science were motor actions. Parlebas classified all the sport practices and concluded that football is a sport where the practitioner has to confront sources of uncertainty which come from the environment, teammates and opponents. This infers that the reality of football is far different from others, as the athletic long jump, where the sportsman faces a much more stable and controlled situation. The relationships with teammates and interaction with opponents develops a peculiar dialogue where the positive intra-group motor communications are mixed with negative inter-group motor counter-communications (Parlebas, in Martín Acero & Lago, 2005a).

In addition to the classical performance components, Parlebas (1988) refers to a series of universals (factors) which act as configuration parameters of the structure of each sport. Hernández Moreno (1994) summarises them in: laws of the sport, technique or execution models, tactics, playing (socio-motor) space, sporting time, motor communication and motor strategy. These universals assign a unique structure to each speciality (Sampedro, 1999). The concrete expression of these structural elements allows developing a more integral vision of the specific competition reality in each sport.

Models to understand team sports have kept evolving during the years going from the classical ones, as the bio-energetic or the praxiologic, to the systemic ones (Sampedro, 1999). The systemic model studies the relationship between the sport integrants and components under the idea of totality, where the modification of any factor affects the performance of the whole system, as it is formed by a group of elements interacting between themselves (Greháigne, 2001). Authors such as Durand (1979), Menaut (1982) or Sanvicens (1984) (all of them in Sampedro, 1999) help to understand the notion of teams as complex systems, supported by the dynamic relationship between elements and the reciprocal interaction between the game and the player. This has a crucial implication for training, which should be open and diverse, designing situations where the player experiments and has different alternatives from which to choose from, even having the challenge to learn from his errors which, ultimately, will improve his decision-making skills under competition stress.

From all of the above, the analysis of the game action in team sports has to go beyond traditional observational procedures and requires the determination of qualitative multi-personal variables (Martín Acero & Lago, 2005a). This idea can serve to illustrate an evolution of the object of study from Mahlo´s (1969) reference book: from the playing action to the playing interaction. We could even go further in the subsequent years and include the playing retroaction as an object of study. From a practical point of view, this means that the action of a player is enriched by the interaction and retroaction with teammates and the environment. Due to its conceptual importance, section I.2 will try to bring light to this approach to study football as a complex dynamic system.

I.2 THE PARADIGM OF COMPLEXITY IN FOOTBALL

It was not until a few decades ago when football became an object of study for sport scientists. The organisation in 1987 of the First World Congress on Science and Football in Liverpool (United Kingdom) represented an attempt to bring together international experts from different sports with a similar code to football (rugby, Gaelic football, Australian rules football, etc.) helping to share and expand the state-of-the-art knowledge. Since then, the number of papers published in peer-review journals has exponentially increased showing a vast interest of different applied sciences (biomechanics, physiology, medicine, psychology, etc.) in football performance. Going through the research studies presented in the seven previous editions of these Congresses, as they have a four-year periodicity, we can find that most of the investigations have been focused on the quantification of objective performance data, whereas very few qualitative studies have been addressed in the literature so far.

If we move from theory to practice and go to watch how elite football teams train nowadays, we can still see plenty of strategies inherited from the Classical Thinking process. Many coaches, especially fitness or conditioning coaches, conceive the footballer as an athlete and believe in independently training his physical capacities and, once done so, put him into the game. The physical development of this universal athlete is based on isolated training programs for each capacity, using fitness tests as an evaluation tool and a reference to feedback the program. In parallel, the skills coach works on the technical abilities of the player, that is, the relationship between the footballer and the ball, which are thought to be the specific components of performance. Once this individualised training approach is concluded for each member of the squad (the player has achieved the aimed fitness scores in the tests and masters the basic skills), all the footballers are put together to work on the team tactics. This traditional mechanistic vision needs to be questioned and replaced with new theories and methodologies more in line with the reality of the game. Analytical thinking, carrying out fitness tests, training physical capacities in isolation, developing athletes instead of footballers or solely collecting quantitative and objective data, appears to be an obsolete approach to modern football.

I.2.1 Foundations of Complex Thinking

The classical perspective to handle research during the twentieth century did not fulfil all the concerns of the different scientific areas. Specifically, the application of reductionism reasoning to biology left many hard questions to answer, unresolved issues which emphasised the need of a new thinking framework (Capra, 1996). The behaviour of human beings manifested properties that could not be studied under the Cartesian-Newtonian approach, that is, only with deterministic concepts and models. Thereby, this ended in a revolutionary break or "paradigm shift" to gain an insight into a better understanding of nature (Kuhn, 1962).

The general systems theory, originated by Ludwig Von Bertalanffy in the second half of the twentieth century, laid the foundations for the application of general concepts and principles in all the systems, independently of their sociological, biological or physical nature (Balagué & Torrents, 2011). The mechanistic prism gave way to a holistic conception of nature and living things, creating new information which was not visible before.

A system is represented by a series of elements which interact between themselves with the aim of reaching a certain objective (Morin, 2000). The characteristics of a system are dependent on the way the elements are configured and manifest four categorical properties: interaction, entirety, complexity and organisation (Durand, 1992, in Martín Acero & Lago, 2005a; Morin, 1982, in Silva, 2008). The properties of a system cannot be explained by individually examining the parts as any change in these parts affects the whole (Morin, 2000). Complementarily, the whole has qualities that the parts do not have in them, which was long ago reflected in the classical Aristotelian holism: "The whole is something more than the sum of its parts". Living organisms represent an example of complex systems, so the comprehension of the interaction and interdependence between their parts allows viewing them as integrated wholes (Capra, 1996).

The development of ecological psychology (Gibson, 1979), structuralism (Lévi-Strauss, 1998) and synergetics (Haken, 1983), among others, opened doors to a new interdisciplinary field of knowledge, where research tools and methodologies could be shared between different areas to build connections which facilitated an integral examination of the human behaviour. All these, at the time, incipient disciplines contributed to the settling of complexity sciences, which have been used to trans-disciplinary study complex systems, providing a theoretical background to understand their behaviour. The French philosopher and sociologist Edgar Morin, one of the greatest references of Complex Thinking, established the essential principles to guide this paradigm, which were summarised by Balagué & Torrents (2011):

- **Uncertainty:** The behaviour of a complex system cannot be predicted over the long-term.
- **Entirety:** The whole is greater than the sum of the parts.
- **Interdependency:** There is an interaction between all the elements.
- **Spontaneous emergency:** The interaction of the elements creates a new entirety which is different from the sum of the parts.

Different names have been employed to address this conceptual revolution: systems theory, systems thinking, systems dynamics, nonlinear dynamics, network dynamics, complex dynamics, theory of complexity, etc. Capra (1996) specifies that systemic is the most scientific term used to define this field, whereas dynamical systems theory is probably the most extended.

Alongside the systemic prism, the ecological worldview is critical to examine living systems, due to their intimate connection with the environment. The concepts of homeostasis and entropy contribute to understand the behaviour of these living organisms. Homeostasis, developed by Walter Cannon in the 1920s (Capra, 1996), represents the ability of self-regulation of a system, whereas entropy is used as a measure of disorder. The reformulation by Ilya Prigogine of the second law of thermodynamics and his investigations on thermodynamical systems far from equilibrium and the phenomenon of irreversibility, that won him the Nobel Prize in Chemistry in 1977, opened a new theoretical framework to understand living systems.

Depending on the fact of exchanging or not exchanging energy with the environment, systems can be considered open or closed, respectively (Martín Acero & Lago, 2005a). Open systems are continuously interchanging energy with the surrounding so they maintain themselves far for equilibrium (Capra,

1996). According to Balagué & Torrents (2011), complexity only exists if both order and disorder are present, as a complex structure is resultant from the lack of equilibrium (Prigogine, in Martín Acero & Lago, 2005a). Thus, complexity deals with this kind of uncertainties and randomised phenomena which determine a mix of order and disorder (Morin, 1994).

The existence of these unbalanced situations permits open systems to adopt different configurations or models of self-organisation (Capra, 1996). This means that a complex system is permanently in a dynamic state, oscillating between phases of order and disorder. The most effective area of the system would be that close to the edge of chaos, as it will allow a greater energetic interchange with the environment. This makes complexity intimately associated with the chaos theory (Tamarit, 2007), which is used to study the behaviour of dynamic systems that are highly sensitive to initial conditions.

The examination of how complex systems self-organise is extremely important. Unlike machines, living organisms have emergent properties and organise themselves following a network pattern instead of adopting a hierarchical structure. This spontaneous emergency reflects new properties and an order in the system which did not exist at a lower level (Morin, 1994). Balagué & Torrents (2011) argue that no matter how much we know about the components of living organisms, without understanding how they interact and create their relationships networks, we will never know about their behaviour. This is why systems thinking concentrates on understanding the basic principles of organisation and of organising relations, as the interdependence between the components is what determines the essential characteristics of a system (Capra, 1996).

Traditional mathematical tools and equations —developed for a linear world —proved ineffective to describe the highly nonlinear nature of complex systems (Capra, 1996). Linear equations could explain hierarchical relationships between variables but were inappropriate to examine network patterns, as these present trajectories which can go in all the directions. Additionally, small changes in nonlinear systems can have major effects as they can be amplified by self-reinforcing feedback (Capra, 1996). Balagué *et al.* (2013) highlight that the discovery of non-linear mathematical equations has aided in describing qualitative behavioural changes in systems. Thus, if we are able to find the general laws that govern organisations, we could then solve problems in all domains (Balagué & Torrents, 2011).

There are many other key concepts as chaotic attractors, dissipative structures, fractals, auto-poietic networks, etc. which are crucial to understand dynamic systems theory but go beyond the objectives of this book. Nevertheless, all the ideas presented in the previous paragraphs can be summarised in the following definition from Capra (1996):

> *Self-organisation is the spontaneous emergence of new structures and new forms of behaviour in open systems far from equilibrium, characterised by internal feedback loops and described mathematically by nonlinear equations.*

In addition to the systemic perspective, the application of synthetic thinking represents an educational challenge at all levels. This is a critical notion as analysis means isolating something to study, while synthesis integrates that thing into a superior whole (Capra, 1996). When we split sport performance into many small pieces we are making the same mistake as when we are overusing a compass in a foggy mountain. If we are constantly looking at the compass for the right direction we start moving in parallel courses and, instead of being closer from our objective, we are farther from it. The same happens with football; as much as we fragment the problem we will never be near the absolute truth, moreover, we will be losing insight from the game. This is because fragmenting does not only imply the separation of the parts, but also the annulment of the properties of a system (Tamarit, 2007). Thus, when the parts of a system are divided one can only acquire knowledge; in order to achieve insight, synthetic thinking is required (Monzó, 2006).

The use of synthesis enables to understand how the parts work together. Therefore, the perspective is now reversed and, instead of focusing on the isolated parts, the essential principles of organisation of the whole are of the main interest. Hence, football needs to be globally understood, as the whole has properties due to the interactions and relationships between its parts and the relationships between the whole and the context (Capra, 1996). It can be that in the subsequent years instead of using the terms 'match analysis' or 'performance analyst' to study, in isolation, the different components of the game, the direction of the process changes favouring understanding the behaviour of complex systems, that is, the interaction between the different elements. This would probable help in developing a holistic vision of football, as the next section will try to show.

I.2.2 Application of Complex Thinking to football

One of the main objectives of the training process is to reduce the uncertainty that the competition represents; that is, coaches try to model their team performance during the week to prepare for match-play. Verkhoshanky documented in the 1970s (Verkhoshansky & Verkhoshansky, 2011) one of the first views of the programming of training as a systemic process. Decades later, several authors as Greháigne *et al.* (1997) or McGarry *et al.* (2002) have coincided in conceiving team sports as complex dynamic systems, which could be studied with tools obtained from the general systems theory (Passos, 2008). Martín Acero & Lago (2005a) also believed that a sporting game represents a complex system as it verifies the principles proposed by Morin (1994): systemic, self-eco-organisation, dialogic, hologrammetric, retroactive loop, organisational recursivity and subject reintroduction.

According to Davids (in Balagué & Torrents, 2011), complexity sciences can be used to efficiently study human behaviour during sport and physical activity. These sciences lay down a differential approach to understand the occurring events in team sports. Additionally, the correct application of the Paradigm of Complexity would mean a great leap to understand team sports and to build their own competition performance theory, leading to new training and methodological developments (Martín Acero & Lago, 2005b). In this sense, ecological dynamics (Gibson, 1979), coordination dynamics (Kelso, 1995) and the network approach (Passos *et al.*, 2011) have been proved effective to increase the understanding of the physical, technical and tactical components of sports and their game dynamics (Balagué *et al.*, 2013).

However, not all team sports have the same level of complexity, as this will be related to the variability of the situations which can occur inside the game

(Martín Acero & Lago, 2005a). At this point, it is important to respect the differences between the terms complexity and complication (Atlan, 1988, 1990, 1991, all of them in Martín Acero & Lago, 2005a; Morin, 1994). A complex situation occurs when we lack important information to manage an uncertain game episode. This does not mean we need more time to solve it, but we need more knowledge than that we have (Ramos Torre, 1996, in Martín Acero & Lago, 2005a). On the other hand, complication is more related with the idea of difficulty and temporal restrictions to find the solution to a situation.

Stepping into the reality of football, we can find complex systems at different levels: players, teams and games/matches. Each of these entities demonstrate the principles of complexity, which need to be respected when studying the phenomena. From the concepts described in the previous section it is clear that footballers should be considered as complex systems, and the same happens with teams, as they are formed by a group of players. In both cases, the whole is more than the sum of its parts and, hence, a footballer is more than the sum of his capacities, whereas a team is different to the mere association of its players (Mallo, 2013).

The football player needs to be holistically conceived, respecting that there is a continuous interaction between all his capacities and between him and the environment (Figure I.1).

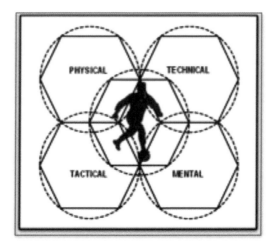

Figure I.1 Relationships between the dimensions of the football player.

This implies that, theoretically, players with worse physical conditions or genetics to play football are able to reach top-class standard as they self-organise their capacities in a different way, empowering other structures to perform in the sport. This is one essential characteristic of complex systems, which are able to develop emergent behaviours to adapt to different contexts. The final solution is never known at the beginning but will emerge due to the complex interactions between all the parts and the environment. Two situations will never be the same as the constraints will always be different, which makes the predictions of long-term performances very complicated (Balagué & Torrents, 2011).

Teams represent micro-societies where network relationships are built between the players (Teodorescu, 1984, in Martín Acero & Lago, 2005a) and can be studied under group dynamic analysis (Castelo, 1999). The studies carried out by Morin (1993) help to clarify this idea, as the relationships between the players create a new collective identity which is different from the independent activity of the players. By doing so, the system shows properties that the elements do not present in isolation in another system. Again holistic, interaction, environment, chaotic, nonlinear behaviour, etc. are auxiliary concepts which help to describe these complex systems.

The alliances established between the footballers of a team can have a multiplying effect on their abilities. This leads to the emergency of a collective behaviour which modifies the individual behaviour or each player. Wilson (2013) illustrates a classic example, in the words of Arrigo Sacchi during his management years at A.C. Milan, to highlight how an optimised self-organisation can be achieved at elite standard:

> *I convinced Gullit and van Basten by telling them that five organised players would beat ten disorganised ones ... And I proved it to them. I took five players: Giovanni Galli in goal, Tassotti, Maldini, Costacurta and Baresi. They had ten players: Gullit, van Basten, Rijkaard, Virdis, Evani, Ancelotti, Colombo, Donadoni, Lantignotti and Mannnari. They had fifteen minutes to score against my five players, the only rule was that if we won possession or they lost the ball, they had to start over from ten meters*

inside their own half. I did this all the time and they never scored. Not once.

It is extremely important to recapitulate the above-mentioned statements, as considering a team as a system reinforces the crucial role of the interaction between the players (Figure I.2), going beyond the traditional match analysis studies based on the independent actions of the footballers. The relationships between the footballers configure game interactions which need to be modelled in order to emerge the pretended collective dynamics, the pattern which the coach wants his team to regularly manifest during the games (Silva, 2008). Thus, the kind of playing that a team achieves stems from the interaction between the footballers (Frade, 1990, in Silva, 2008) and these relationships can have a different meaning depending on the entirety that is finally generated (Silva, 2008).

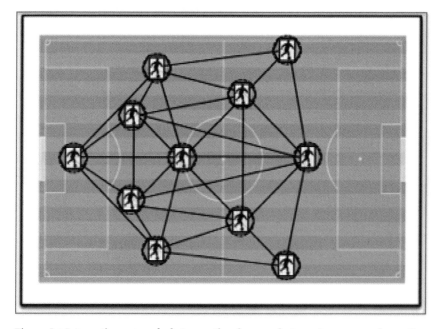

Figure I.2 Interaction networks between the players of a team in a 1-4-3-3 formation.

The process to achieve a new organisation is not immediate, as the system —team— has to go to through unstable phases until, finally, a more effective organisation emerges. Balagué & Torrents (2014) highlight that the players need to practice this new collective behaviour in training in order to stabilise it. This behaviour should be stable but not automatic, as it requires flexibility to adapt to the different training situations. Additionally, the ecological perspective needs to be respected and the team has to be viewed as an eco-system, due to its intrinsic relation with the environment. In this sense, the team has to be able to adapt its structure and function to the tactical constraints of the competition game.

The varied performance showed by top-class players when playing for their home club or their national team has been a frequent topic of debate for journalists. Lionel Messi has been subjected to these kinds of discussions when comparing his performances at FC Barcelona versus the Argentine national team. How can the performance of a player be so different when playing with different teammates? Complexity sciences will probably yield new tools for people to understand Messi´s role in both eco-systems.

When we look deeper into daily football issues we can find coaches who configure their team line-up around the necessity of balance, searching for a perfect equilibrium supported in quantitative parameters. Therefore, if the coach wants to use two players in front he selects a tall one (1.90 m) and a short one (1.70 m), so he averages the "optimal" stature (1.80 m). This strategy is repeated in other positions: one offensive fullback and one more concerned on defence; a fast player on one wing and one with a greater endurance on the other; a midfielder able to play long balls and another accurate in short passing; a central defender good in high balls and another one fast to cover his back, and so on. Interestingly, in elite football the extremes, and not the average values, are distinctive. This is why Valdano (in Suárez, 2012) warns:

> *Football is full of nested sentences but no one knows whether they are true or not. It seems mandatory to play with a midfielder who runs, as clumsily as he can, because the important thing for him is to gain the ball back and to sweat.*

The day FC Barcelona and Spain´s national team broke with all this fictitious sense of control they won all the major trophies at club and national team level, respectively. How could they achieve this if they did not respect the conventional rules to build a team? One of the explanations could be that by altering the traditional thinking they became unpredictable for the opponents. This represents an outstanding characteristic to optimise performance in team sports, as it is not essential to have ideal players to be able to produce a playing style with exceptional qualities (Balagué & Torrents, 2011). Argentinian Marcelo Bielsa is a clear example of a coach capable of producing successful teams (Newell´s Old Boys, Vélez Sarsfield, Athletic Bilbao, Olympique de Marseille, Argentina and Chile national teams) which prioritise collective playing over individualities.

In addition to football players and teams, the game can also be considered as a system (Greháigne, 2001), as different elements interact with the objective of winning the confrontation. Probably, the first coach to apply a systemic approach to football was Ukrainian Valeriy Lobanovskyi. Lobanovskyi studied engineering in the USSR where he came in touch with cybernetics. Years later he met the statistician Anatoly Zelentsov and set the basis for Dynamo Kyiv´s success during the 1970s and 1980s. Their scientific principles, thoughts and procedures were included in the book "The Methodological Basis of the Development of Training Models". Wilson (2013) explains how Lobanovskyi interpreted football:

> *Football eventually became for him a system of twenty-two elements —two sub-systems of eleven elements— moving within a defined area (the pitch) and subject to a series of restrictions (the laws of the game). If the two sub-systems were equal, the outcome would be a draw. If one were stronger, it would win ... The aspect that Lobanovskyi found truly fascinating was that the sub-systems were subject to a peculiarity: the efficiency of the sub-system is greater than the sum of efficiencies of that comprise it ... Football, he concluded, was less about individuals than about coalitions and the connections between them.*

When two teams begin a football game there is an initial state of balance. If both teams just have order, there will be no space for creativity and thus, the system —game— will continue in equilibrium (draw). To unbalance the situation a team has to increase its energy interchange with the environment to produce unexpected situations for the rival. Thus, a game represents a continuum dialogue between the teams, alternating between phases of order and disorder with the objective of breaking the stability of the opponent.

This infers that a game of football is built with unpredictable and indemonstrable events, which makes it impossible to go back and re-test alternative hypotheses. Therefore, there are no identical situations so every time a player makes a decision or a coach selects a team, he can be right or wrong, but there would never be another chance to test different solutions in a twin context. The game is a continuous loop where every situation influences the following, creating a series of events without a logical sequencing (Oliveira *et al.*, 2007). There is a constant co-adaptation of all the dynamic systems to the game requirements, as one player or a team influences the other one and *vice versa*. In addition, everything that a player or a team does affects the environment (referee, crowd, score, etc.) at the same time as the environment has a reciprocal influence on players and teams. It is not the same playing home or away, a friendly match or the World Cup final.

Match-play situations also raise interesting questions, why do some teams perform better when one of their players is sent-off? How can it be possible to improve the outcome with 10 rather than when 11 players? This represents another practical example of an optimised self-organisation. When the system — team— loses one of its members, it has the capacity to create a new organisation in order to adapt to the situation. This is one of the main characteristics of dynamic systems, which machines are unable to possess. The case of players that form part of the squad helping the team to have a better functioning and performance, despite never appearing in post-match statistics and television interviews should also be highlighted. These kinds of players improve the team harmony, as they optimise the communication and organisation networks by producing emphatic behaviours which help emerging associative synergies between teammates. This is very important and should be a major concern for performance analysts, as many of the data registered during the match only reflect descriptive parameters which do not help to obtain a good comprehension of the game dynamics and the real individual and team performances.

Figure I.3 shows a simple illustration of the systemic notion discussed in the previous paragraphs. Each player, in isolation, is a complex system. When the players train together and share a common identity and tactical background they end up forming a bigger system: the team. When this team confronts an opposition team, a greater complex system is generated: the game, which can be subjected to multiple sources of stress (referees, crowd, media, etc.). Each of these systems form a whole with respect to its parts while at the same time being part of a larger whole, becoming a fractal, as the structures are repeated at inter-related scales (Davids, in Balagué & Torrents, 2011; Pol, 2011). When we move from one level to another the properties of the systems change, as each level has its own laws and organised complexity (Capra, 1996). Both ends of Figure I.3 could even be expanded. On one side, the systems, structures and capacities which compose the footballer could be studied in depth. On the opposite extreme, a detailed analysis could be carried out regarding what happens when different matches are collected together, as in during a league competition or a cup tournament.

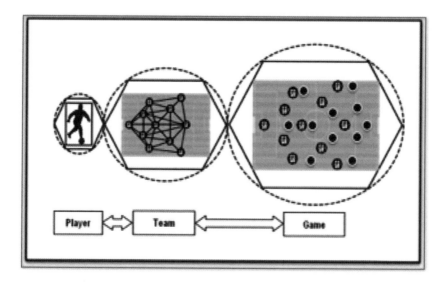

Figure I.3 The player, the team and the game as complex systems. There is a fractal relationship between them: each system is contained in the following level of organised complexity.

A system can be examined from two different perspectives which are intimately related: structure and function (Durand, 1979, in Silva, 2008; Martín Acero & Lago, 2005a). The structure represents the rigid and static side of the system (Morin, 1982, in Silva, 2008), whereas the function represents the relationship between the elements. When examining a team, its structure would be characterised by the playing formation. However, more important than this playing formation is the way the elements of the system —footballers— interact between themselves when the ball is in play. Hence, this game dynamics is the functional organisation of the structure (Silva, 2008). The selection of a playing formation should help the development of positive game dynamics between the footballers of a team.

With a wider perspective, Garganta (1997) also proposes the use of a systemic prism for the analysis of the game. The structural analysis of football would be represented by its characteristic elements: the player, his direct opponent, teammates, direct opponent teammates, space, time, ball and the rules (Martín Acero & Lago, 2005a), whereas the functional analysis will try to bring light to the study of the confrontation between the two teams. Capra (1996) believes that function is a mechanistic concept whereas organisation is a better representation of systemic thinking. Therefore, it is essential to define and describe the different organisation levels that the football game system might have (Greháigne, 2001).

As it was previously explained in section I.1.3, we can identify different subsystems levels (Martín Acero & Lago, 2005a). The smallest level, micro-system, is represented by the attacking and defending activities of players under 1v1 situations, which can be defined as elementary duel episodes. When more than one player from a team come together to develop cooperative strategies, with or without the ball, meso-systems are found. These partial duel episodes reflect group confrontations involving dyads (2v2), triads (3v3), overloaded (4v5) or unloaded (6v4) situations. Finally, team macro-systems or complex networks can be described when the totality of the team is involved, as it happens during competition (11v11), which is categorised by Martín Acero & Lago (2005a) as a dual conflict episode.

Martin Acero & Lago (2005a) use these three organisation levels to clarify the ideological differences between the reductionist and holistic perspectives.

Reductionists focus on the smallest levels of the scale, trying to explain the system behaviour from the elementary individual player confrontations. Thus, it is more important to have good players in a team rather than the playing formation and tactical relationships potentiated by the coach. On the other hand, the holistic approach prioritises the upper side of the scale, the macro-level. In this sense, the interaction between the players inside the playing system is more important than the capacity of each player on its own.

At the end of the day, it is crucial for coaches to optimise both of the complex systems, the football player and the team. During the last few years, increasing attention has been paid to examine synchronies at individual (player) and collective (team) scales (Duarte *et al.*, 2013). The development of compound positional variables as geometrical centres and team ranges (Lames *et al.*, 2010) or stretch index measures (Yue *et al.*, 2008) and the application of complex mathematical tools and algorithms (Duarte *et al.*, 2012; Frank & Richardson, 2010; Richardson *et al.*, 2012) might provide a new insight to study the synergies of players and teams during match play.

We can question plenty of situations which occur on a day-to-day basis in a football setup and are solved using a Classical Thinking strategy, but could be confronted with Complex Thinking reasoning. Starting from an individual — player— point of view, many people fragment the training components and believe fitness is the critical indicator of performance. This has led to the acceptance of several universal syllogisms in the football domain in an attempt to predict physical match performance. As a consequence of this, the score in selected fitness tests have been related to physical match performance (Krustrup *et al.*, 2003, 2006) and, hence, if a player improves his fitness, he would obtain a better score in the tests and, ultimately, he would be able to produce more intense exercise in the course of a competitive match. Therefore, the necessity of certainties for coaches has resulted in applying fitness test to predict if a player (or a team) is going to be able to run in the last stages of the match, forgetting all the other constraints that can affect the behaviour of complex systems.

Going beyond the statistical presentation of the test data, when performance in fitness tests is correlated to minutes played at the end of the season, the results are contradicting. Furthermore, if a conditioning coach classifies all the players from a squad according to their fitness values (objective classification based on the tests scores) and the head coach does the same using the criterion of football performance (subjective classification founded on what the player produces under a football context), we would probably find a low correlation between both variables. How can this be possible in modern football? Why do players who do not achieve the best scores in fitness tests are more relevant for team performance than those who stand out in off-the-ball running, squatting and jumping activities?

Similarly, performances in physical and technical tests are employed to select young players for football academies. Physical tests could be used as an adjacent tool to control maturity and development, but never as a unique criterion to decide whether or not a footballer would progress into a superior standard of competition. It is very common to see elite clubs or national youth teams (specially containing players aged 15 to 18) formed by excellently physical developed footballers although, when those players reach 22-23 years old and should be playing professionally, they are out the game. Thus, short-term performances of physically mature players are placed above the long-term development of talented players who understand the game. Clubs and football associations should ask where their money is invested in youth football, as they are paying high salaries and giving scholarships and socioeconomic benefits to players backed by their physical development without having football talent. Years later they have to pay transfer fees to get back players which had been discarded because they were smaller, weaker or physically immature in comparison to those selected.

The reductionist and holistic approaches can also be examined by assessing if training contents are focused on the player (action) or on the team (interaction). As stated earlier, for the last few years there has been an over-exaltation of the role of the physical component in performance and teams that show higher distance covered in post-match statistics are thought to be fitter. This has led many coaches to benefit the cult of the muscle forgetting about the decision making processes. However, in most of the situations it is not about running more but knowing when to run. A team with a good organisation makes the players look faster, as they will always arrive at the ball in the right moment, giving the false sensation of being fitter. In this sense, the key issue is not developing the best physical condition as possible, but to enhance the tactical intelligence of the players, which makes them capable of getting the most from their capacities, learning to interact with teammates and opponents and, in summary, understand the game. Therefore, training must not be based on the repetition of exercises, as the learning process requires an intention in the action to achieve a real educative purpose (Oliveira et al., 2007). This sets a critical difference in the conceptual framework: training the muscle versus training the brain.

It should not be read from the above that physical condition is not important in modern football. It is obvious that possessing a superior maximal oxygen uptake, being faster or jumping higher is better than not doing so. The question is how these values should be improved or, more specifically, is it really important to increase these parameters in isolation or is it more appropriate to favour the development of the game insight?

As we are working with open and dynamic systems, we will never have complete evidences about the real transference that out-of-the-game activities have on football specific situations. Is it effective for a central defender to do four sets of six repetitions of squats to improve the heading of the ball? Again, the syllogistic reasoning is clear: heading depends on jumping; jumping (explosive force) can be improved by squatting; therefore, if a player improves his rate of force development when squatting, he would improve his heading. But do things work as simple as this in nature? Or are we using this simplistic reasoning to make us feel more comfortable with what we are doing in training? If we only have 90 minutes of training time per day, would it be more effective for the players to dedicate half of the session to lift weights in the gym or to carry out specific (tactical) training tasks? It is common sense 45 minutes of strength training is better that not doing so, but the question is, should this kind of training be done during the team training time? Many fitness coaches will have more respect from players and coaches (most of them, former footballers) if they dedicated more time to understand the game rather than on displaying all kinds of apparatuses on the field. In a certain sense, it would be similar to swimming; nobody would design a training program for swimmers based on non-water activities. The specific adaptation is critical to achieve top-class standard in all the sports.

Pep Guardiola, reinforces the previous idea by explaining that all the training exercises carried out at FC Barcelona under his management included the most important tool: the ball. Thus, football players are required to be familiarised with the game, developing cooperative relations with teammates to achieve common goals and competitive relations with opposing players, and the only way to achieve this is by training with Specificity (Oliveira *et al.*, 2007). In the last circumstance, it would be up to the manager the kind of player or team he wants to develop. If being intelligent is more important than the physique, then training tasks should stimulate the autonomous decision making skills in the footballers.

Players who have been little exposed to specific decision making situations or have been trained following linear progressions in closed environments, have problems when they confront challenges away from the remote control of the coach. These footballers can even become blocked when they face unknown situations, not knowing what the next step to take is. In elite level football, there are many times when the coach is unable to quickly contact the player (because of the crowd, noise or distance) and the player has to take the tactical decisions on his own, in order to position himself adequately. The only way to facilitate these processes is by designing specific and significant training tasks, to prepare the player to be continuously thinking during the game, identifying game situations and anticipating what is going to happen. By doing so, the player is ready and capable of solving tactical problems that might arise during the matches, reacting faster and tacking advantage from his rivals.

From all of the above, it is important to highlight the importance of the Paradigm of Complexity to understand the direction that performance methodology in football should take in the future. Martín Acero & Lago (2005b), supporting themselves in Prigogine (1993), discuss that team sports training pathway should be built among two different tendencies that lead to failure if they keep on acting independently. On one hand, certainty theories are characteristic of the deterministic conception of team sports but are far away from practice. On the other, empirical theories are based on field situations but lack from reflection as they are founded on the immediacy of the moment. The combination of theory and practice, reflection and action, should aid creating a better approach to football training. Therefore, the CV of modern coaches must be interdisciplinary, integrating the art and science of training methodology and group management skills (Mallo, 2013).

The systemic training perspective prevents isolating the parts to examine what is happening inside them and the independent treatment of the performance components (physical, technical, tactical and psychological). Additionally the moments of the game (organised attack, organised defence, attack-defence transition and defence-attack transition) form part of a continuum and cannot be divided into separate parts, as if attacking and defending were two different entities. Even though, in many texts, the words phases and moments of the game are interchanged, Oliveira (2004) considers that the term phases reflects a sequential order of the events, whereas the moments of the playing can be randomly manifested during the game. All the moments of the game are interlined and while the team is in possession of the ball (attacking moment) some of the players are already thinking on the defensive moment, being close to their opponent just in case the team loses possession. Thus, the collective and individual playing tempo is manifested when the team is able link consecutive sequences (attack, defence, transitions) without them appearing isolated episodes. The same happens at individual level; a footballer shows a high playing pace when he is able to concatenate, in the competition specific context, different actions and interactions in the benefit of team performance.

It is important to clarify that integral or integrated training (García Manso, 1999; Tschiene, 2002) is not the same as training based on complexity principles (Torrents, 2005). Integral training theories have greater biological, analytical and static properties, whereas complex training has a wider and holistic conception of the process, with dynamic and emergent properties and showing an interest in how the systems interact between them (Balagué & Torrents, 2011; Solé, 2002; Torrents, 2005). The training drills can be a fractal from the game if they include the characteristic collective dynamics. If they only contain isolated parts, they cannot be considered as fractals since they will not meet the Specificity of the game (Oliveira *et al.*, 2007; Silva, 2008). Due to their importance, these concepts will be further detailed in section III.5.

During the subsequent chapters two different applications of Complex Thinking in football will be presented. Both of them share a holistic perspective of nature but focus on different systems: Paco Seirul·lo´s vision of the sportsman as a functional unit and Vítor Frade´s "unshakable integrity" conception of the game. Altogether, Seirul·lo and Frade will provide an innovative approach to examine football training, confronting many of the traditional principles which have been universally accepted under the classical football axiom "this is who things have been done in the past" or the ancestral law of the instrument which says, "If all you have is a hammer, everything will look as a nail" (Maslow, 1966). Therefore, it is time to shift the traditional football view and open new thinking avenues; if football is a complex phenomenon, it has to be studied with complex tools.

©Real Madrid C.F.

PART II

SEIRUL·LO´S STRUCTURED TRAINING

*"The human being should never set a limit to his sport performance.
A model is setting a limit"*

Paco Seirul·lo

II.1 THE ORIGIN: PACO SEIRUL·LO

Any discussion about FC Barcelona´s training methodology must never forget to mention one figure: Francisco "Paco" Seirul·lo (Salamanca -Spain-, 1945). Despite FC Barcelona´s international reputation being identified, as it names suggests, to its success in football, it is very important to praise the multi-sports philosophy of the Club. In this sense, its five team sports professional sections (football, basketball, handball, futsal and roller hockey) have won, by the end of the 2013-2014 season, a total of 36 European Cups —which is the best continental trophy haul at club level— with each team having won the competition at least once. To enhance the grandeur of the club, 89 national League and 91 national Cup trophies complete the impressive honours list. Complementarily to these professional sections, FC Barcelona involves a variety of amateur sports as field hockey, ice hockey, rugby, volleyball, athletics, figure skating and wheelchair basketball.

In fact, one of these disciplines —athletics— was Seirul·lo´s route of entry into professional sport. After finishing his Physical Education degree in 1972, he taught athletics in the National Institute of Physical Education (INEF) of Madrid between 1972 and 1974, in combination to teaching duties in other Faculties and Sports Associations. Indubitably, Seirul·lo´s teaching career is associated with the INEF of Barcelona since its foundation in 1976. For almost 40 years he taught Kinesiology, Motor Learning, Training Theory and Planning, or Foundations of Physical Education, in the Degree, Master and Doctorate courses held at this Faculty (Martín Acero, 2009). This vast theoretical experience led him to the publication of a great number of manuscripts covering a wide range of sport topics, with many of them having been used in the elaboration of this chapter of the book (as an example, Seirul·lo, 1979, 1986, 1987b,c, 2003, 2009).

Along these 40 years Seirul·lo took his training thoughts to practice in a variety of sports as athletics, volleyball, judo, tennis, motorcycling, handball or football, preparing athletes and teams for Munich ´72, Montreal ´76, Los Angeles ´84 and Barcelona ´92 Olympic Games and for nine additional World Championships (Salebe, 2011). His first job placement at FC Barcelona was in the athletics section, between 1976 and 1984. In 1982 he became the fitness coach of the handball´s first team, holding this position until 1996 and, some years later, he joined the Spain national handball team, winning the World Championship in 2013. His professional relationship with FC Barcelona´s football section started in 1994 and, many years later, he still is considered the principal reference in relation to training methodology (Martín Acero, 2009). In this period he has worked with managers as Johan Cruyff, Sir Bobby Robson, Carles Rexach, Louis van Gaal, Lorenzo Serra Ferrer, Radomir Antic, Frank Rijkaard, Pep Guardiola, Tito Vilanova and Gerardo Martino, winning 9 Leagues, 4 Cups and 8 Supercups at national level and 3 UEFA Champions Leagues, 1 UEFA Cup Winners Cup, 3 UEFA Supercups and 2 FIFA Club World Cups at international level. As an additional fact, in May 2006 he became the only coach to win the football and handball Champions League —European Cup— in the same season.

During the transition in his professional life from individual to team sports, Seirul·lo detected multiple contradictions and inconsistencies which took him to open new avenues for training and research. As early as 1976 Seirul·lo published a paper predicting the way that training sciences should take in the future and introduced terms as synergy, systems or optimising training times, which were incipient at that stage (Seirul·lo, 1976). Together with colleagues from the INEF of Barcelona he has been working on this direction during the last decades, searching for a specific training methodology for team sports different from that applied in individual sports.

From a practical point of view, Seirul·lo was surprised to witness the same kind of activities as those carried out in athletics in his initial experiences in team sports, "Starting from a low position, 'On your marks, get set' ...and sprinting 5 or 6 times 25 meters" which made him reflect, "I have never seen a player in a team sport standing still, waiting for an acoustic stimulus to run in a straight line without anybody bothering him" (Seirul·lo, in Palomo, 2012).

Many coaches considered that as football included running, jumping and kicking/throwing, athletics should be the training foundation of the players (Seirul·lo, 1999). The conception of the footballer equivalent to an athlete has been extended worldwide, though it represents a reductionist approach to understand him, as Panzeri anticipated as early as 1967. Seirul·lo has also been critical with this idea in several occasions, requesting a profound change of perception and thinking.

> *It was thought in the past, erroneously, that the first thing was to develop an athlete and then he could play whatever sport. If endurance was desired to be developed, it was equally trained in the mountain, in the sea... wherever. And then that endurance was adapted to the sport. And that is not true. That way you lose time and energy, as every sport requires its specific treatment. (Seirul·lo, in Cappa, 2007)*

> *Once it was said that, first of all, we have to develop athletes and then footballers. I have been training athletes, sprinters and throwers for a long time. If you develop an athlete, he will really be an athlete. The boy since the age of six has to be a footballer and has to learn football's specific motor abilities, football's spatial-temporal conditions, interpersonal relationships, the emotion of the game of football, the traditions and wisdom of the game of football. First developing an athlete and then changing him into a footballer is very difficult. He will never feel it as much as the first case. From the beginning he must be a footballer. (Seirul·lo, in Palomo, 2012)*

The quantifiable conception of the footballer is a legacy from the Classical Thinking, where teaching —focused on the mind— was based on behaviouristic theories and training —focused on the body— was based on what could be measured, providing an atomised and multidisciplinary model (Seirul·lo, 2002). This Cartesian, constructivist and mechanistic perspective was a characteristic feature from individual sports and was extrapolated to football, instituting the bioenergetic and the biomechanic phenomena as the principal performance axis (Seirul·lo, 2000). Hence, the observed behaviour of the player was the matrix of the process, evaluating what the player did during competition and what he was capable of doing when tested (Seirul·lo, 2000). To improve his playing capacity closed drills or "pedagogic/exercise progressions" were designed (Seirul·lo, 1999), with the aim of taking the player from a known starting point to a known finishing point. Thus, training contents and systems were designed for each capacity critical for match play and performance was evaluated through fitness tests, which were used to feedback the process. This way, sport was understood from a rigid point of view, prioritising the vision of the human being as a machine, as the following quote from Seirul·lo (2000) demonstrates:

> *I find the publication of VO_2max data from footballers very funny. The efficacy of the greatest observational laboratories of these physical phenomena is ±2-3%. The data which we are given after a blood test presents a high reliability of ±2-3% and are considered as valid. Nevertheless, if we go to a player and say, 'If you are 2% late where the ball is...' 2% less in 3 m is outrageous! And we think it is scientific because there is a science, analytical, which has established a code in which ±2-3% represents a high reliability and we say, 'We are in the limits of scientific reliability.' There is no point in that, because we are using a linear observation methodology in nonlinear methodologies and phenomena and that is not good enough for us. We have to give support to other sciences in the scientific structure of team sports. We have to observe them from a different perspective. Our interest is what happens in each sportsman after creating appropriate environmental conditions; the importance is what happens inside the player, not the external modifications we can observe.*

Seirul·lo (2005a) reinforces the previous ideas by arguing "we cannot use instruments that describe linearity or phenomena based in linearity, to approach the investigation of nonlinear problems and systems" and justifies the necessity of a change in the conception of training. Thus, the use of logic progressions and the search for the maximisation of capacities where "more of the good is always the best" (Seirul·lo, 2005b) has given way to an epistemological opening where individual sports traditional principles and laws are no longer valid for team sports.

In order to highlight the special features of team sports, Seirul·lo (1998a) anticipated the following critical aims which were needed to be respected during the training process:

- Great control of the training workload.
- Enhancement of performance with a low number of sessions.
- Variation of contents so that training is attractive for the player.
- Easy assimilation of training contents due to the proximity of competitions.
- Maintaining the sporting shape of the players during all the competitive period.

The complex and inter-systemic interaction conditions which circumscribe collective sports, where two teams simultaneously participate in a common space, must be examined, always respecting the holistic, chaotic and randomised game characteristics (Seirul·lo, 1999, 2005b). Altogether, this creates a peculiar scenario in which (Seirul·lo, 2005a):

> *The player [in team sports] has to be a highly specialised spectator, at the same time as being an actor, as he has to observe the specific signals emitted by his teammates, the object and his opponents; at the same time as interpreting a complex role by means of languages and meta-languages which need to be correctly interpreted by his teammates, incorrectly by his opponents, aesthetically well valued by the spectators, validated by the referee and accepted by the coach as compatible with the proposed tactical plan.*

The foundations of complex behaviour allowed Seirul·lo (2000, 2012) to establish this new paradigm to study team sports. Structuralism understands the human being as a hyper-complex structure, away from the preterit conception of isolated compartments. Therefore, all the systems which make up the human structure are continuously interacting between themselves, creating a dependent relationship network (Seirul·lo, 1999). This provides a different approach to team sports training and, though it was not originated in football, it can be of enormous benefit when applied in it (Seirul·lo, 2005b), as Seirul·lo (in Palomo, 2012) affirms:

> *I cannot understand fitness isolated from football. Everything to be done on the field, understood as physical conditioning, has to be linked with football and with tactical and cognitive interests. Traditional fitness enhances physical condition with weights, sprints, running on the beach, in the forest. In my opinion, that kind of conditioning for football is not valid, does not exist. Fitness has to be integrated with the totality of football training. Talking in traditional terms, technique, tactic, fitness and psychology all has to be one. Fitness cannot go on its own with nothing to do with football´s gestures, football´s spaces and football´s interpersonal relationships.*

Seirul·lo has influenced a great number of football coaches and fitness coaches. Lorenzo Buenaventura, former FC Barcelona and current FC Bayern München fitness coach under Pep Guardiola´s management, is probably one of the most relevant practitioners of Seirul·lo´s methodology, as Perarnau (2014) shows:

> *Buenaventura learned the Structured Microcycle methodology from Seirul·lo, which is based on short training cycles, three to five days long, which are dedicated to one physical capacity: strength-endurance, elastic strength or explosive strength, depending on the player and the moment of the season. Training simulates the technical and tactical conditions of the next match, always with the ball. That is, you train as you play. The game principles proposed by Guardiola are present in each minute of training.*

Alongside with understanding the sportsman as the reference of the process and developing a specific training methodology for team sports, Lago (2009) believes that the third great contribution of Seirul·lo to team sports training has been developing a functional training unit: the weekly micro-structure. Due to their conceptual importance, all of these key elements will be thoroughly explained in the following pages.

II.2 A TRAINING METHODOLOGY BASED ON THE PERSON (THE FOOTBALLER)

II.2.1 The person and his (self-)structuring as the referential axis of the process

Seirul·lo´s training philosophy is based on gaining insight into the sportsman, who follows a unique optimisation process (Seirul·lo, 2000). This sets a crucial difference with other methodologies whose references are the sport, as Seirul·lo (2001) explains:

> *If our starting point is the observation of the game as a model, we are committing a serious mistake, as all the game models are situational, even if we take an ideal model developed by the coach. Thus, the methodology must be adjusted to what the person is capable of doing.*

Consequently, the importance lies on what takes place inside the sportsman rather than what happens outside (Seirul·lo, 1993). The development of neuroscience, information theory, systemic thinking, systems theory, ecological theories, cognitivism or structuralism during the last few decades has provided tools to study complex behaviours during team sports practice. In this sense, the human being is self-organised throughout the interactions and retroactions of different systems that form the following structures (Figure II.1; Seirul·lo, 1998a, 2000, 2002, 2005b,c, 2012):

- **Bioenergetic:** Substrate utilisation to support activities.
- **Conditional:** Traditional physical capacities and values.
- **Coordinative:** Execution of specific skills.
- **Cognitive:** Information treatment and processing.
- **Socio-Affective:** Interpersonal and intergroup relationships.
- **Emotion-Volitive:** Self-identification against our intentions and desires.
- **Creative-Expressive:** To facilitate self-projection in our environment (field of play).

• **Mental:** Enables putting knowledge together.

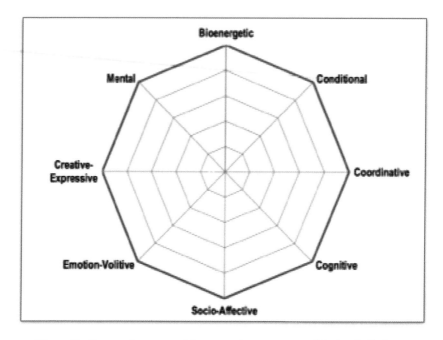

Figure II.1 Interaction network between the structures of the football player (after Seirul·lo, 1998a, 2000, 2002, 2005b,c, 2012).

All these structures are continuously interacting between themselves to generate a hyper-complex structure which is the footballer. It is very important to highlight that these relations follow a network pattern and not a pyramid, as it was traditionally understood. We do not develop ourselves with elementary building blocks but with connections and, therefore, any activity carried out by a player is the expression of inter-systemic relationships under a structural conception of the process, as Seirul·lo (2000) exemplifies:

> *A player jumps, controls the ball, lands and always takes one step to the front. We teach him exercises to control the ball with the chest; running, controlling the ball with the chest and passing it back to the player in front, five players facing each other. The top-*

level sportsman will say that this [kind of exercise] is old, whereas the starters will have great problems with it, as each system needs an optimising and own self-stimulation process.

In one of his first studies on this topic, Seirul·lo (1999) explained that, at least, conditional, coordinative and cognitive structures should be simultaneously involved during training in team sports. Even though training tasks can have a preferential direction, they must implicate other structures, as every activity carried out by a player is the product of the interaction between different complex systems (Seirul·lo, 2000).

Physical capacities represent sectorial evaluations of a system from a structure (Seirul·lo, 2002). All the different physical capacities are optimised to configure the physical condition of the sportsman. Seirul·lo (1998a) distinguishes endurance, strength and speed as the three basic conditional capacities, from which strength is the most important in team sports (Seirul·lo, 1998b). Each of these capacities shows a different manifestation in each playing position and every player gives a different importance to them in his self-structuring process (Seirul·lo, 1990). In addition, there are other conditional facilitating capacities as flexibility and relaxation.

As mentioned above, these physical capacities are worthless in themselves, as they need to be developed in interaction with coordinative and cognitive capacities (Seirul·lo, 1998a). Coordinative capacities support the specific skills of football players and are necessary for driving the ball, passing, shooting, etc. (Seirul·lo, 1999). Seirul·lo (1998a) provides a very detailed classification of coordinative capacities, which can be organised into a first (movement control capacities), second (spatial movement implantation capacities) and third (temporal adequacy capacities) level. Cognitive capacities are used to integrate and process external and internal information, conjugating all the other capacities to provide the best solution to each game-specific situation, in other words, optimising the interaction between structures.

The influence of cognitivism and structuralism is critical in Seirul·lo´s training organisation and differs from the preterit conception of considering the human being as a machine. The sportsman is formed by a network of structures whose optimisation allows solving a certain situation in various ways. Seirul·lo

(2000) believes that training and learning strategies should not be based on repeating movements, but providing the player with different experiences which lead to information exchanges between his systems and the environment. This variability will allow him to create new self-structuring schemes and self-optimising his systems towards the final sporting movement. This gives the process a unique characteristic, as if a system belonged to a different structure, it would work in a different way (Seirul·lo, 2000). The case of Pep Guardiola, as a football player, can be used as an example of this interpretation of the person, signified by the words of Johan Cruyff (in Suárez, 2012):

> *I still remember when they told me, when I arrived to Barcelona, that there was a boy in the academy who technically was of the best. Why is he not playing for the reserves or for the Under-19s? I found him playing for the Under-18s. The excuse was the same as always: he was physically weak. I told the Club to promote him to the reserves and to make him play in a position with greater requirements. As he felt valued, he took a leap. If you do not create expectations to the academy boys, you are killing them. In addition, the weak have developed a special intelligence, the ability to find alternatives, because if you do not do it and you collide with someone, you are lost. You learn from your own body. It happened to me. I was not strong.*

Guardiola (in Suárez, 2012) recognises his physical limitations and explains his adaptation from playing as a winger to a midfielder:

> *If you do not adapt, you will not survive. As I had a weaker physique than the other players, I had to think faster, touch the ball quicker and not collide with other players. That way you are unconsciously developing yourself, adapting to your deficits. If at any time I collided with another midfielder or defender, it was because I had done something wrong, that was obvious.*

Thus, as previously indicated, attention has to be placed on the person, on what happens inside the player and not what we externally observe (Seirul·lo, 2000). The internal processes of the player, and not the external factors as traditionally conceived, are in charge of this "differentiated structuring" and the self-modelling (Seirul·lo, 1998a). By training his own resources the player will, ultimately, optimise his potentialities (Seirurl·lo, 2003). Auto-structuring by "differentiated optimisation" can be achieved by (Seirul·lo, 2002):

- The establishment of technical-tactical abilities in which the player is competent.
- The observation of the influence of competition on the player.
- The constant acquisition of insight about the game, training and himself.
- The generation of the self-social image in situations that require from social interaction.
- The achievement of game insight by the player during practice using technology and research tools.

Consequently, training tasks must expose the footballers to nonlinear and variable conditions, which are essential to create an effective learning process. Nonlinear systems are based on creating successive unbalanced situations (Seirul·lo, 2000). When the initial and final characteristics of the environment are modified, the player has to elaborate new solutions as a reaction to his personal relationship with them. On the other hand, if we are always using identical kind of training contents, the structures will be in equilibrium and the player will always use the same systems to solve the situations, losing prospective power (Seirul·lo, 2000). Thus, it is essential to provide training variability to the footballers to safeguard the maximal prospective power of each of the systems. By doing so, the player can configure his own systemic structuring to solve the game situations in different ways. On a long-term basis this is critical as (Seirul·lo, 2000):

> *The talented subject who has been built up in this way, even without knowing it, can create different solutions than the majority of players, because his self-structuring pathway has been varied for each of his systems.*

This is a key characteristic of top-class players, who are in an imbalance point as they have not been trained with linear models. For instance, these players can respond like an open and nonlinear system and "that is why on many occasions, talented players do not listen to their coaches and do not listen to us, because they see we are not valid for what they need" (Seirul·lo, 2000). The development of the player can only be achieved when all the structures are progressing evenly (Seirul·lo, 2002). Therefore, training systems should be adapted to the specific necessities of the players in every moment of their sporting life (Seirul·lo, 1999). The following reflection from Valdano (in Suárez, 2012) can be used to summarise this section:

> *If you try to systematise a genius, you take the risk of killing his creativity. Mechanisation enhances players with lower skills but sinks the creative ones. However, it is very difficult to damage players as Messi or Agüero, as they are personalities who have survived all the processes. When they arrive to the First Team nobody can change their playing pattern.*

II.2.2 The foundations of Structured Training

The self-structuring capacity of the sportsman is essential to understand this new training conception of team sports, which has been also known as Microstructuring, Structured Microcycle (Seirul·lo, 1998a, 2001) or, more recently, as Seirul·lo´s Cognitive Model of Synergistic Functionality (Martín Acero *et al.*, 2013). Under this perspective, the sportsman is formed by an interaction of structures, systems inside systems, which built up a high complexity network where all the elements are in reciprocal connection (Seirul·lo, 2002, 2005b). Thus, Seirul·lo rejects the use of the classical closed, linear and repeated exercises in football training, which are meaningless in his methodology as he shows in the following answer from the year 2000:

> *I will tell you that in the five years I have been in FC Barcelona [In the first team of the football section] we have not carried out a single steady state run more than 6 minutes long, even in the preseason. Players never go out to run 40 minutes in the forest; never. We have never done fartleks in our life. Fartlek is an athletic*

training which has been adapted to other things, but it is an athletic training, suitable for athletes. Reaction speed in individual sports is useless for collective sports.

All the proposals in Structured Training should be based on the sportsman (Seirul·lo, 2003). Thus, training must provide situations where the different structures and systems of the footballer interact between themselves and adapt to the specific sporting context (teammates, opposition and environment). When a footballer confronts a new training situation, his development is not based on how he repeats a given response but on how he is able to organise his structures to solve these challenging circumstances. This determines a training direction which Seirul·lo (2002) refers to as "prioritised" rather than "hierarchised." The optimisation of all the capacities and structures will enhance his future development as a footballer (Seirul·lo, 2001).

These training micro-situations can be prioritised or oriented to preferential conditional capacities such as strength, endurance or speed. This can be done by managing the number of repetitions and sets, the recovery periods between exercise bouts, the intensity, etc. In addition, the contents must request the participation of the coordinative (specific sport abilities) and the cognitive (information processing and decision making) structures. When the coach follows these postulates to organise training, he is building specific training systems for team sports (Seirul·lo, 1999).

The process by which a person finds a solution to these high variability practical situations is unique, as every sportsman generates particular self-organisation strategies in order to reach greater self-structuring stages during his sporting life. Therefore, it is a very individual procedure and each footballer has to assume responsibility to lead his learning process. The progression to higher standards of competition will be dependent on the prospective power of the footballer, that is, his ability to manage the capacity to self-optimise his performance through dynamic inter-activities (Seirul·lo, 2002). To clarify these ideas, nothing better than reading how Seirul·lo explained in the year 2012 the way Andrés Iniesta reached his level of excellence:

> *Since he was 12 years old he was here, in 'La Masía' [FC Barcelona residence for young players] and, until last year, he has done nothing for his conditional structure. His own biology and specific practice has given him the possibility to get where he is today without doing any strength, speed, endurance, flexibility... and you will say: Is this untrue? It is true!!! What does it mean? That by being very weak and with a limited endurance, little fast and little of everything, in the sense of little that all of you have, he has 'hypertrophied', optimised for us, his cognitive, coordinative, emotional, etc. structures. He enjoys making a good assist or passing to keep possession more than scoring a goal. These are the values he has been using all his life, so when we now ask him to take one step further to apply this against any opponent or situation, he just needs to understand how his opponent is and what he, together with his teammates, can propose in his game. Because in team sports, the greatest problem in competition is who is in front, his evaluation will give us the reference on what to do to overcome him and to create unknown situations for him. This allows showing a high competence in the game development, as Iniesta does in such an 'apparently' easy way, to edge over the opponents and to build the kind of play that each moment of the game requires.*

Javier Clemente, former Spain´s national team manager between 1992 and 1998, continues explaining Iniesta´s special virtues as a footballer (in Suárez, 2012):

> *You see him and say: 'He is a dwarf that you can throw to the ground with a simple blow.' Conversely, you don´t know the number of ball possessions he regains, and that many people don't notice it. He doesn't do it because of his physique, he intercepts by his position. He doesn't collide because he lacks stature, but he doesn't need it. He just has enough with anticipating.*

Finally, Iniesta gives his own view on his development as a player despite his physical limitations (in Suárez, 2009):

Since I was a child I knew I would never have an important physique, but I have never felt inferior on a field because of that. The head is what commands. You are not going to recover more balls by being taller or stronger. Football needs more from intuition than from the physique. You do not always need to strongly dive to the ground.

As it was indicated in the previous section, Pep Guardiola, in his years as a player, was another example of a footballer who potentiated other structures to survive in top-class sport. Perarnau (2014) describes how Guardiola was a physically weak player, without defensive virtues, so he had to "guess the following pass even before receiving the ball, train his body to facilitate the technical gesture and base the strength of his game in passing to support his teammate." Seirul·lo (2000) used another practical example to further explain his views on this topic in a question and answers round during a congress in the year 2000:

If I tell you that the fastest player at FC Barcelona is Guardiola, will you believe me? I do one speed training per week and the player who best resolves the speed situations, with the components I demand, is Pep. Sergi [FC Barcelona's left back at that moment] is much faster than him in 5 to 20 m, stopping, accelerating... but if before they start they have to solve a problem, during the execution they must see the position of the teammates to choose which direction to go to and they need to finish in a certain position on the field, Guardiola is the first.

From all of the above, training should not be directed to selectively potentiate a certain structure or system, as the traditional conditioning methods have pursued and instead should promote and stimulate new interactions between structures, optimising the capacities of the player in accordance with the competition standard. It is not about getting the most from an isolated structure, but making all the systems interact, retroact and to synergic collaborate to reach a superior self-structuring (Seirul·lo, 2012), respecting which has been known as the Principle of Synergic Action (Seirul·lo, 1998a). In order to achieve this self-organisation, Seirul·lo (2005b) emphasises that training must respect the following characteristics:

- We never have a scientific certainty of the initial level of the player. This is why the variables and capacities must not be maximised but optimised; optimising the systems interactions will lead to optimise all the structure.
- Structural changes are only possible when the structures have a variety background, which allows creating interconnections with the other structures and systems.
- We have to take the players through a configuration way where we cannot define, aprioristically, the future of the player. This pathway should be specific and close to total specialisation, that is, continuously ensuring that the systems of the player are out of equilibrium, so there is an energetic interchange with the environment.
- This configuration way is irreversible, so we cannot go back through it as there will be a residual shaping trace on the player.

II.3 PLANNING IN FOOTBALL

II.3.1 Definition of planning

Planning tasks in a collective sport like football must be considered inside a wider context: the sporting project. The external circumstances are always providing feedback to all action plans, so the coach needs to manage as many variables as possible. Among the features which help to configure the project of the team, Seirul·lo (2001, 2005b) recommends identifying the history and cultural environment of the club, its functional organisation, the players and staff socio-economic conditions, the objectives of the season, the calendar of competitions and the available training facilities and technologies. All of these circumstances will have an impact on the type of players, manager and coaching staff to hire, as everything must be related to create a style of play in accordance with the philosophy of the club.

Once the characteristics of the sporting project have been concreted, the next step will be to plan the process. Following what was shown in the previous sections, planning in football must respect the intrinsic complexity of the sport. Traditional plans based on individual sports have no place in football, as everything has to be referenced to a complex environment: changing interactions between systems, qualitative spatial-temporal relationships, high variable and nonlinear context, undetermined and randomised game episodes, etc. (Seirul·lo, 2002, 2005b). Seirul·lo (2001) clarifies his outlook to this topic by saying:

> *Individual sports planning, and team sports as an extension, contains closed proposals. A particular player is intended to adapt to 'the player' which has been, theoretically, developed by a group of experienced coaches who, under the justification of science, are proposing it as an ideal model of player to take part in that sport. They argue that the player who adapts to this model is the one who performs in the sport. In other words, the player model is constructed from the sport, as a result of how certain coaches interpret the sport, assuming that their interpretation is unique, is the best, without realising that in the majority of the cases they*

> *are doing it with the experience accumulated from a successful player or, at best, from a group of players that achieved success following that model developed by him or by his group, without realising that the only players who succeed with him are those that, by mere chance, have a very similar bio-structure to that model. All the other players, they argue, are not valid for that sport. Consequently, many disciplined sportsmen have been wasted, as they strictly followed plans which were not appropriate for their capacities.*

According to the foregoing, the football planning epicentre must be located in the actual player and not in data from previous performances, that is, using external references or values from ideal footballers. The structures of the player are always in a dynamic unbalance, so the player has to be in charge of directing himself through the self-shaping processes during his sporting life (Seirul·lo, 2005b). Hence, the aim has always to be focused on the footballer, on how he is able to continuously optimise his systems inside his own interpretation of the sport (Seirul·lo, 1998a).

Seirul·lo (2005b) defines planning as "foreseeing and sequencing all the training events which are needed in team sports." These training events include all the practical situations such as exercises, sessions, competitions, recoveries, medical and fitness tests, holidays, etc. In other words, everything the player does while he is under the structure of the team. It is not just about reaching an optimal shape and maintaining it during several games, as it has to provide continuous adaptation challenges in the search for qualitative improvements during all the sporting life of the footballer (Seirul·lo, 1998a). A recent opinion from Seirul·lo (in Palomo, 2012) is useful to understand his basic principles about planning:

> *The process I am talking about, to understand football in this way, is not carried out in one season. It represents a philosophy of understanding the game, a little bit like Barcelona´s philosophy. The team identity is concretely defined by the type of players and the philosophy that the environment entails, in which those players are. If the training dimension encourages something which is*

strictly not that, things get complicated. If we have a physical condition adjusted to what the player needs, it can be maintained all the season. For that purpose, strength and speed endurance are the predominant qualities, in fundamental terms. These types of qualities are easily recovered and can be trained all the year. On the other hand, if we did the 'traditional, endurance' training cycle we will have lots of problems to maintain it all the season. The competition load is very high, with three matches per week and if, additionally, we needed to train endurance we will be slowing the displacement forms that the players require in this kind of playing. We always have the tendency to work a short time in training, but always at a very high speed. These elements are always optimised with very few repetitions and longer recovery pauses. With real game situations played on reduced spaces. This gives you the chance of being in a good shape all season long.

II.3.2 The concept of sporting shape in the footballer

As Seirul·lo´s training methodology is based on the person, it is very important to define the notion of sporting shape, as it has a great influence on the configuration of the training scenario. Seirul·lo (2005b) believes that getting in shape is not just about the physical side of performance, neither overdeveloping a single capacity or a structure. Football does not work in this way as the aim is to continuously optimise the dynamic interaction of all the structures, without maximising the development of only one of them. Under this holistic approach, the sporting shape of the team sportsman has to be observed from the following prisms (Seirul·lo, 1993, 1998a):

- **From the individual perspective of the player.** All the systems of the player must be optimised, working together to give solutions to the problems which might arise during each game and enhancing individual performance inside the team setup.

- **Regarding teammates.** There should be a homogeneous sporting shape within all the players of a team, to ease interactions between players and apply the collective playing style and particular playing systems.
- **Regarding opponents.** During a season there will be confrontations with plenty of rivals in different competitions, for example, in national and international tournaments. Each opposition team will have different individual characteristics and collective styles of play which need to be considered and studied.
- **Regarding the moment of the season.** Team sports habitually present a very long competition period which, in the case of European football, can be 10 months long. During the season a team can take part in different tournaments with diverse formats: league, cup (knock-out competitions), play-offs, etc. Thus, each moment of the season can require a different level of sporting shape according to the objectives of the team. Seirul·lo (2001) adds that these solicitations can also be influenced by the social expectations of the environment, as when confronting a team with a great rivalry. This highlights the importance of conceiving the sporting shape of a team under an ecological framework; it is impossible to abstract it from the cultural environment and social pressures.

The characteristic long competition period of football does not allow manifesting the principles of traditional periodisation models where peaking coincided with the moment of the season with the highest density of important competitions (Matveiev, 1964, 1977). Therefore, Seirul·lo (1987a) references Bompa (1984) to define three different levels of shape in which the footballer could be in the course of a season:

- **General sporting shape:** Principally linked with a high development of all the physical capacities, that is, with the accumulation of generic training volume.
- **High sporting shape:** Characterised by the implementation of specific (technical and tactical) training contents, which lead to adaptations related to the particular sport.

- **Optimal sporting shape**: Represents the maximum level which the sportsman can achieve, where conditional, technical and tactical values are optimised inside the specific sport context.

Ideally, it would be interesting for the footballer to be in this last (optimal) level as long as possible during the season. However, it is difficult to implement this in practice as it impossible for a footballer to maintain an optimal shape during a nine or ten months long competition period (Seirul·lo, 2001). Due to this limitation, footballers should be in the second level —in a high and sub-optimal sporting shape— during most part of the season, raised up to the optimal level in three or four selected moments (Seirul·lo, 2001). The way the load dynamics is organised has to facilitate these inter-level transitions, applying synergies between training contents at the same time of avoiding the use of generic workloads (Seirul·lo, 2005b). In this sense, Verkhoshansky´s block training system (Verkhoshanky & Verkhoshansky, 2011) and Bondarchuk´s (1988) ideas of relating conditional, technical and tactical components were used by Seirul·lo to develop his training organisation model.

As performance in team sports depends in the cooperation and interaction of different players, the concept of sporting shape cannot be limited to the analysis of a single individual. Hence, the coach has to develop a great awareness of the situation to be able to develop sporting shape synergies between the players of his squad. The adequate stimulation of all the footballers will fine tune the interaction between themselves to optimise collective performance. This is why Seirul·lo (2001) suggests the use of Structured Training or Micro-structuring to achieve the expected results in team sports, as he has been experiencing for more than 30 years.

II.3.3 Characteristics of planning in football

Seirul·lo (1998a, 2005b) identifies four major characteristics which football plans should have: unique, specific, personal and temporised.

Unique

The fact of planning being considered unique reflects the necessity to converge all the thinking and action strategies from the people who are directly involved with the field performance of the team. In this way, the different possible points of view between members of the same coaching staff about how to understand the training phenomenon must be discussed. This will ensure the adoption of a uniform criterion to provide the footballers with unequivocal proposals (Seirul·lo, 2005b). Moreover, these training tasks must be consistent with the project of the team, implementing a congruent training methodology in accordance with the playing philosophy of the club, without this meaning to copy external models. Seirul·lo (in Salebe, 2011) refers to how this process occurred in FC Barcelona in the following commentary:

> *Barcelona´s football, since the last 20 years when Johan Cruyff was there, has been following a specific learning methodology for a way to play football and a philosophy to carry it out. This process does not happen in a few days, as it requires long time, and starts with 14, 15 and 16 years old boys. When these players are 20, 22, or even less, and move to the First Team, they manifest the school and formation to play this dimension of football.*

Under the perspective of Seirul·lo (1998a, 2005b), the unique planning notion has an unavoidable budget which is conceiving the person as a hyper-complex structure. This is why training has to be focused on optimising all the structures and systems, through the interactions between them.

Specific

As its name suggests, planning has to be a consequence of the particular characteristics of each sport. The laws of the game and the rules of each competition set the singular properties of football, which implies that the training contents cannot be transferred between different disciplines. Seirul·lo (1998a, 2005b) lists the following features to emphasise the importance of developing specific plans in football according to:

- How the player interprets the internal logic of the sport (after Parlebas, 2001).
- The interpretation by the player of the environmental space of the competition: referees, family, supporters, members of the board, etc.
- The management of the number of competitions, training sessions, recoveries, travels, etc. during the season.
- Achieving success in the most important competitions of the season, as reflected by the objectives of the team.
- The rules of each competition regarding the number of players which can be involved.
- The organisation of each individual competition, player management and minutes to be played.
- The previous results in competition and the expectations towards the following matches.
- The characteristics of the next opponent in competition.
- How the player accepts the decisions of the referees during the game.
- The way to plan the training sessions, combining group and individual stimulus. Seirul·lo (2005b) highlights that, despite carrying out collective sessions, the player must feel as if training was focused on him, to satisfy his own demands.

All of these factors have to be taken into account by the coaching staff when designing a specific plan, in order to be able to increase the quality of the training proposals to allow the inter-systemic optimisation of the player. It can be worth trying to evaluate the initial situation of the players according to the previous epigraphs, to identify their shaping level in each moment of their sporting life (Seirul·lo, 2005b).

Personalised

Again, the hyper-complex notion of the sportsman is privileged here. Everything to be done during training has to consider the person inside the sport. All the personal structures are a reflection of the underlying processes, which create a dynamic network relation between the systems (Seirul·lo, 2002). In this sense and as previously indicated, what we traditionally know as capacities only represent partial evaluations of the processes that account in a system from a structure (Seirul·lo, 2002). This implies that the progression of a sportsman can only be achieved when all the structures are evenly developed.

Seirul·lo (1998a, 2004, 2005b) recommends respecting the following three criterions before designing a personalised training plan:

- **Personal sporting talent:** This is not the isolated demonstration of excellence in one capacity, as it requires a systemic interpretation. Personal talent must reflect the interaction between all the structures.
- **Sporting life project:** Figure II.2 summarises Seirul·lo´s long-term development phases for team sportsmen. Each phase's ages and duration must be adapted to individual situations. It is extremely important not to leapfrog the initiation phases, as the players will eventually lose prospective power having done so. This is not just a reference classification as it has a decisive effect on the planning purposes. Thereby, it is essential to determine in which moment of his professional life the player is in when planning.
- **Differentiated integration:** This last criterion reveals the importance of putting together the internal values of the player (talent and sporting life) with the game and the environment. That is, training has to provide events which facilitate the integration of the player in the structure of the team and all the playing alternatives of the team in the player (Seirul·lo, 2005b).

Seirul·lo's Structured Training

Age (yr)	Phase	
5	Initiation to Practice	Unspecific regular practice (5-7 years old)
		Multi-purpose general formation (8-10 years old)
		Oriented multi-lateral preparation (11-13 years old)
16		Specific initiation (14-16 years old)
17	Acquisition of High Performance	Specialization (17-19 years old)
		Fine tuning (20-23 years old)
28		Stability and high performance (24-28 years old)
29	Decreasing Functionality	Conservation of performance (29-34 years old)
		Compensatory adaptation to performance decrement (35-38 years old)
41		Functional re-adaptation for non-competitive performance (30-41… years old)

Figure II.2 Long-term development phases of team sportsmen (after Seirul·lo, 1998a, 2004, 2005b).

Temporised

This final planning characteristic aims to sequence all the events which are proposed during training (Seirul·lo, 2005b). As Figure II.3 shows, this temporal organisation can be referenced in four levels which, on a general basis, will be explained in this section and, on a specific context related to Structured Training, developed in section II.4.

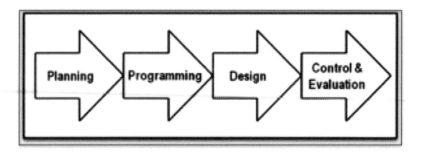
Figure II.3 Temporal sequencing of the organisation of the training tasks.

Planning tasks are the first ones to be carried out and mark the establishment of a hierarchy and a temporal administration of objectives (short-, medium- and long-term), the playing style and systems, the involvement of players in competitions and the division of the season into periods. As it will be further explained in the next section, Seirul·lo (2005b) divides the season into three periods: pre-season, competitive season and transition, each of them sub-divided into structured microcycles, which are the principal characteristics of Seirul·lo´s yearlong training plan.

The second level corresponds to programming tasks which represent the training organisation strategies. In this sense, they include shaping sequences and preferential simulation situations (also known as potential simulation situations in Seirul·lo, 1993), which must be selected in accordance with the structures of the players to be optimised and the desired style of play of the team. Figure II.4 represents the hierarchical relationship between them which will be further examined in section II.4.2. The pretended effect of these situations is to optimise the individual and group subsystems performances, directed towards the consecution of the team collective outcome (Martín Acero & Lago, 2005a).

In combination with programming tasks, design tasks help to implement the weekly and diary practical training conditions so that the players can specifically perform inside the sport (Seirul·lo, 2005b). This includes the temporal (total duration, exercise duration, pauses and recoveries between drills, etc.) and spatial (equipment, groups, number of players, etc.) organisation of the session.

The way the contents are designed will have an impact on the kind of socio-affective relationships developed between the players, so it is an essential aspect that the coach must consider.

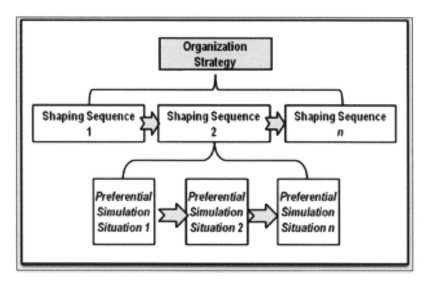

Figure II.4 Relationships between organisation strategies, shaping sequences and preferential simulation situations in Structured Training (after Seirul·lo, 2000, 2002, 2005b).

Finally, control and evaluation tasks are used to provide feedback to the process. Even though these terms are interchanged in some texts, Seirul·lo (1993) differentiates between them. Control tasks are used to determine the effects that the training process has had on the sportsman, at the same time as assessing the effect of each type of training in the functional systems of the person (Martín Acero & Lago, 2005a). Evaluation tasks are more related to competition, examining how the systems of the player behave under the maximum stress situation: the game. In a sport like football these tasks require high doses of creativity, to find appropriate methodologies to obtain meaningful data from training and competition and to subsequently treat that data in order to provide results to enrich the whole process.

II.4 THE PROCESS OF STRUCTURED TRAINING

Seirul·lo's interpretation of sports training found shelter under complexity sciences, based on the cognitivist and structural vision of the human being which locates the person as the centre of the process. This creates a distinctive approach to the phenomenon in relation to the traditional postulates defended by the general theory of sporting training. Seirul·lo reinforces the separation from the classic maxims by employing a different terminology to define his master guidelines for team sports training. The closed, rational, analytic, reductionist, linear, competitive, quantitative, homogeneous, maximising, stable, repetitive and predictable characteristics of individual sports are opposed to the main features of collective sports: open, intuitive, synthetic, holistic, nonlinear, cooperative, qualitative, heterogeneous, optimising, variable, changing and unpredictable (Seirul·lo, 2000, 2002, 2005b).

In the face of such great differences, the extrapolation of training arguments from individual to collective sports reveals plenty of incompatibilities. This is why Seirul·lo proposes a new approach to team sports: Structured Training or Structured Microcycle. This solution was adopted after years of experience working with individual and team sportsmen and has a profound background in professional football, as Seirul·lo explained in the year 2011 (in Salebe, 2011):

> *[Planning in football] is very complex and complicated as there are between 65 and 75 fixtures during a year and this requires a very good organisation of the training process. It is a job we have been doing since a long time ago in what we call Structured Microcycle, which translates to a weekly control, and that week is related to the previous and the following one. This way, we can better adjust the loads, the training times and recovery in keeping with the specific necessities of the next match, because many times we only have two or three days between matches. We are under these conditions most of the weeks. It is a very detailed workload control process to relate each microcycle with the previous and*

the following ones. After 15 years of working with the First Team, everybody has been collaborating to adjust the work.

II.4.1 Planning tasks in Structured Training

With the objective of achieving a qualitative theory and practice of team sports training, Seirul·lo (1987a, 1998a, 2005b) combines some of the characteristics which have been explained in preceding pages. The main condition of the season plan is Micro-structuring (Seirul·lo, 1998a). Under this approach, the year is divided into three periods according to the calendar of fixtures: pre-season, competition and transition. The week, Structured Microcycle, is the strategic relationship unit inside these periods, as the player has to optimise his structures to perform at an adequate level during one or two days inside this weekly reference (Seirul·lo, 2001). These microcycles are interrelated by different organisation strategies and arranged in shaping sequences (Seirul·lo, 2005b).

To achieve interactions between the sporting shapes of all the footballers there is a proposed load distribution for the different periods of the season. These training loads are related to their similarity with the competitive action and can be considered as generic or specific (Roca, 2009). Specific loads can be further classified into general, directed, special and competitive (Seirul·lo, 1998a), which show an influence from Bondarchuk´s (2007) concepts. Altogether, these categories enable to establish five levels of organising the training loads which present the following main features:

- **Generic:** These kinds of activities are basic and distant from the sport. As an example, a generic task could be represented by football players carrying out a rowing session during pre-season to improve their aerobic endurance.
- **General:** These contents are more related to competition than the previous ones, but are focused on physical capacities in isolation (strength, endurance or speed) and there are no decision making requirements, as when doing running sets around an athletic track or the football field.

- **Directed:** This third level incorporates specific coordinative elements and unspecific decision making processes, as it happens when a footballer drives the ball in a circuit on the field. Contents in this category could be related to the playing position of the footballer.
- **Special:** In this case training activities show a greater similarity with competition, including specific technical and tactical components that demand decision making abilities on the footballers. For example, a 4v4 small-sided game.
- **Competition:** This last level partially replicates competition requirements, as it happens during an 11v11 game in ¾ of the field where the coach searches for the acquisition of certain tactical principles.

When planning by Micro-structuring, training loads are administered on a concentrated way (after Verkhoshansky, 1990). This idea was influenced by Seirul·lo´s findings during his work and research with athletes back in 1973, where sprinters that concentrated their loads manifested better performance improvements than those who used linear stimulation (Seirul·lo, 1987a). This workload dynamic, in terms of volume and intensity, is not directed at physical capacities in isolation but privileges a selective orientation towards a group of systems, searching for their optimisation. The training aims must be focused on adjusting the sporting shape of the players according to the importance of the competitions, always related to the teammates and to the standard of the opponents. Altogether, this should satisfy the individual requirements of the footballer in a certain moment of his sporting life, at the same time as seeking an efficient optimisation process during all his development phases (Seirul·lo, 2005b).

Pre-season period

The aim of the preparatory period, which is habitually between four and six weeks long for European top-class football teams, is to prepare the player for the first competitive fixture. Since the beginning, this period is organised in weekly microcycles with concentrated loads. Seirul·lo (in Cappa, 2007) defined his views on the organisation of pre-season by saying in a press interview:

Seirul·lo's Structured Training

I think it is impossible to fill the footballers' tank for all the season, as it is pretended, just by training one month. Impossible. And us, coaches, have to punish ourselves for this, because we have given too much importance to pre-season. Doing double and triple training sessions during two weeks is not good for the players. You are only punishing the players and they will be paying for it during the first five league games. I feel the right thing to do is only prepare for the first match. Exclusively. And then for the second one, and so on. You cannot organise pre-season training three times per day during two weeks without touching the ball. That damages and it is not useful.

Seirul·lo (1987a, 1998a, 2005b) defines theoretical workload curves for the different parameters for each of the periods in which he divides the season. This training orientation places quality above quantity and this is why the curves have no scalar values in the x and y axis, as these values need to be individually adjusted for each situation. Figure II.5 shows the proposed load distribution for the pre-season following this methodology.

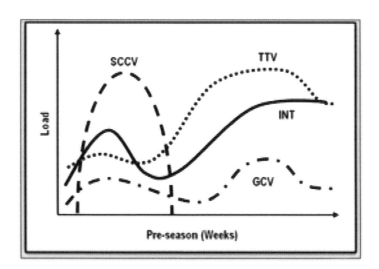

Figure II.5 Training load dynamic during the pre-season. SCCV: Specific Condition Concentrated Volume; TTV: Technical Tactical Volume; INT: Intensity; GCV: Generic Condition Volume (after Seirul·lo, 1987a, 1998a, 2005b).

As Figure II.5 illustrates, the first weeks of the pre-season are characterised by a predominance of Specific Condition Concentrated Volume (SCCV). This volume includes general, directed or special training loads and, according to Seirul·lo (1998a), can occupy 45-50% of the total duration of the pre-season. Technical and Tactical Volume (TTV) acquires relevancy in the second half of the period and comprises special and competitive tasks. These training activities have to be focused on all the structures of the players. In this second half of the pre-season is when the team takes part in a greater number of friendly matches, in which all the footballers should be progressively involved (Seirul·lo, 2001). Generic Condition Volume (GCV) presents the lower values during all the stage and is formed by generic tasks which are used for recovery, to buffer the most stressful loads, or with a control or evaluation purpose (Seirul·lo, 2005b). Finally, Intensity (INT) should increase during the first few days until SCCV reaches its highest value and, thereafter, shows a delayed progression in relation to TTV. This training load distribution should help to estimate the behaviour of the generic and specific shape curves in a similar way to those shown in the graph from Figure II.6.

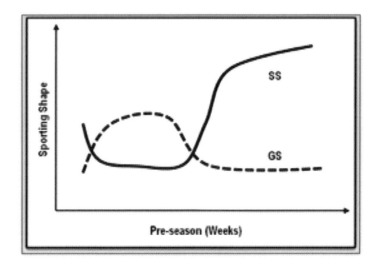

Figure II.6 Theoretical representation of the evolution of the Generic Shape (GS) and Specific Shape (SS) of the footballer during the pre-season (after Seirul·lo, 1998a).

Competitive period

The competitive period, which can be around 40 weeks long, maintains Microstructuring as the functional unit. The training load organisation depends on the number of competitive matches played per week. In the case the team is only involved in a match per week, for example playing on a Saturday, Seirul·lo (1998a) and Roca (2009) propose organising a directed and special concentrated Season Block (SB) in the first half of the week, with a double session on Tuesday and a single session on Wednesday morning, as shown in Figure II.7. When the competitive fixture is on a Sunday, the SB is delayed and concentrated on Wednesday (double session) and Thursday (morning session). The Technical and Tactical Volume (special and competitive tasks) and Intensity curves will progressively increase during the week, reaching their maximum values on its second half, whereas Generic Condition Volume will have a greater predominance after demanding efforts (recovering from the previous competition and after the concentrated training block).

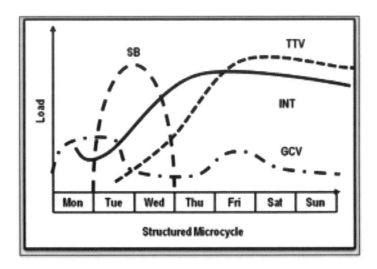

Figure II.7 Training load dynamic of the Structured Microcycle during the competitive period. SB: Season Block; TTV: Technical Tactical Volume; INT: Intensity; GCV: Generic Condition Volume (after Seirul·lo, 1987a, 1998a, 2005b).

This kind of organisation allows the application of specific loads during the week, which help the footballers to achieve fast adaptations curves. Specific training loads principally include general, directed and special training tasks. It must not be forgotten that the official fixture of the week (competition) is the most specific component of the microcycle load (Seirul·lo, 2005b).

The graphical representation of the workloads distribution during pre-season and the Structured Microcycle inside the competitive season (Figures II.5 and II.7, respectively) shows a very similar pattern. The main difference between them comes from the temporal duration of the training cycle, sharing both organisations common principles. Thus, while pre-season searches for the optimisation of performance towards the first competitive game (at the end of the preparation period), the Structured Microcycle looks to enhance performance in the weekend match.

With a season-long perspective, volume and intensity will always show undulating curves, without stable values (Figure II.8). Respecting this undulating characteristic, training volume will progressively decrease during the season in relation to the number of matches in which the team is involved (Seirul·lo, 1998a).

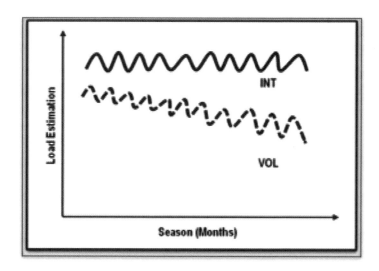

Figure II.8 Theoretical evolution of the Volume (VOL) and Intensity (INT) curves during a season (after Seirul·lo, 1998a).

Transition period

This period connects two consecutive seasons and it is, habitually, around four to six weeks long. During these weeks the players can use generic training loads (as swimming or cycling) which deviate from the specific football requirements. The principal aims of this period are to recover from the overall demands of the previous season and to regenerate the stressed body structures, in order to continue their optimisation during the following training stages.

II.4.2 Programming tasks in Structured Training

This is, probably, one of the most important sections to understand the singularities of Seirul·lo´s training methodology and refers to the conditions to design the training systems and sessions (Seirul·lo, 1998a). The guiding principle in this should be the analysis of competition from the point of view of the sportsman. This is a critical difference with traditional training conceptions where competition analysis was focused on the final outcome. In the actual context, what is happening inside the person, how he copes with the competitive episode is essential. Hereby, competition affects all the structures of the footballer and not some of them in isolation (e.g. conditional), as it has been justified sometimes.

The coach needs to have a profound game insight to detect and extract potential learning situations for the footballers from the competition. In addition, he has to respect the playing philosophy of the team, which influences the kind of experiences to provide the footballer with. Even the player can be involved in this stage, helping to select and design problems and challenges which he frequently faces inside the sport (Seirul·lo, 2002). Hence, all the training proposals must be based on the necessities of the footballer when playing (Seirul·lo, 2001). Each of these situations will be characterised by the presence of diverse conforming elements, which shall recall the interaction between different structures and systems of the footballer (Seirul·lo, 2002). Not all the game related activities will have the same impact on the players, as each of the above-mentioned situations will depend on how the footballer self-configures his structures.

As a result of the interpretation of competition by the player and the coach, training should seek to partially reproduce some of the conditions which configure the real game scenario. The reduction of the distance between training and competition will facilitate reaching new levels of self-organisation. In order to carry out this objective the coach, in harmony with his coaching staff, has to develop the organisation strategy of the training elements (Seirul·lo, 2005b).

The introduction of a new training nomenclature by Seirul·lo accentuates the uniquely of his approach, showing a clear influence from Edgar Morin (1994), who uses the term strategy in opposition to program. A program is a sequence of predetermined actions which, under known circumstances, allows achieving the expected objectives. Thus, everything inside a program operates with automatisms. The use of the term "training program" has been widely extended in sport's learning and training processes. However, it should be highlighted that it has been traditionally identified by the creation of a closed pathway in which the sportsman is positioned, taking him from a known starting to finishing point. This occlusion searches for the generation of stable conditions, so every sportsman that follows the same program will reach an identical concluding state. Under the classical paradigm, training follows a linear sequence with a progressive application of the workloads and always searching for a maximisation effect, taking an established model as a reference to guide the process and which to compare the results with.

The concept of strategy is much richer and can be applied to unstable environments. A strategy is not as rigid as a program and requires a great plasticity, taking into account all kind of external elements. Seirul·lo´s philosophy is not based on certainties, as we are unable to exactly determine the initial conditions of the footballer in the moment we apply training. In addition, we cannot be precise regarding how the ultimate configuration of the footballer will look like. It is for this reason that Seirul·lo (2005b) prefers the use of the concept of "organisation strategy" rather than "training program." The organisation strategies aim to provide the footballer with qualitative training proposals which help the optimisation of his systems and structures, at the same time as being specific to football as these micro-situations extracted from competition replicate certain conditions of the game.

Organisation strategies must have an inter-systemic functionality and contain the basic criteria to temporally organise the shaping sequences (Seirul·lo, 2005b). Each strategy can combine different sequences with their own order of application. The strategies should search for a preferential direction, that is, for the optimisation of a selected system, ideally under a synergic inter-systemic interaction (Seirul·lo, 2005b). The coach has to validate each of the strategies according to the competition requirements, giving them a specific terminology.

Shaping sequences represent the practical circumstances that the footballer must experience (Seirul·lo, 2005b). The term shaping reflects a configuring effect and thus, these shaping or configuring sequences involve different systems from a structure or the development of relationships between structures of the footballer. The characteristics of shaping sequences are determined by the combination of preferential simulation situations, which will be explained in the subsequent pages.

Shaping sequences are specific to team sports and equivalent to what the general training theory knows as "systems" and/or "methods" (Seirul·lo, 2005b). These traditional training systems and/or methods represent closed recipes, as they are designed to be applied on a sportsman whose initial conditions are known by setting fixed conditions on the elements (Seirul·lo, 2005b). For example, if a footballer has a VO_2max of 55 ml/kg/min and we want to increase this value, we can recommend an interval or intermittent training method to improve his aerobic power to him. The foundation of shaping sequences is the opposite as, instead of being cemented on strict parameters and focused on a single system or structure, they incentive behavioural variability (Seirul·lo, 2005b). Hence, they represent combination of training contents which shape some of the structures of the footballer (conditional, coordinative, cognitive, etc.) to achieve a greater self-organisation. In addition, they always have to respect the playing style of the team.

The open properties of organisation strategies are achieved by the combination of pre-fixed and post-fixed elements (Seirul·lo, 2005b). Pre-fixed elements, which represent the fixed side of the strategy, are sequences of elements which have been previously proven to be effective in different kind of footballers and circumstances, that is, elements which are related to the practice of football. On the other hand, post-fixed elements are variable and introduced after examining the outcome of the pre-fixed situation. Once the footballer has concluded the sequence, the coach assesses what has happened and adjusts the conditions in order to create variations in the practice in accordance to the actual necessities of the footballer. The inclusion of post-fixed elements creates new energy interchanges between the player and the environment, altering stable conditions so the footballer has to constantly re-organise himself to solve the situations (Seirul·lo, 2005b). This is a feedback to ensure that the organisation strategies are preferentially optimising (and not maximising) the expected systems, allowing the individual adjustment of the footballer to the situation and ensuring different interaction patterns (Arjol, 2012; Seirul·lo, 2005b).

The coach can design multiple variations of these sequences, in accordance with the characteristics of the player and the style of play of the team. This will create a strategic unit which could contain pre-fixed sequences, which have been previously identified as valid and appropriate for a certain player and team, and post-fixed sequences, appropriate for the unstable conditions of each player (Seirul·lo, 2005b).

Arjol (2012) affirms that there will be no progressions in the sequences but variation in the elements which form them. This means that each player will use his systems in a different way and this interaction will allow him to reach new self-organisation levels. Shaping sequences should be changed in every training session and not be repeated more than two or three times under identical circumstances, as the same situations will never occur in competition (Arjol, 2012). This can be achieved by using post-fixed elements. Complementarily, there will be infinite combination of the elements, but only those related with the playing style of the team and the player necessities will be selected by the coach to be used in training (Arjol, 2012). In addition, Seirul·lo (2005b) sets out some organisation rules which must be respected before programming shaping sequences:

- The same sequence cannot be repeated in a microcycle.
- An identical endurance preferential optimisation sequence cannot be used more than three times in a season.
- An identical strength preferential optimisation sequence cannot be used more than twice in a season.

- Almost identical sequences can only be repeated with a five microcycle separation, should their aim allow doing so.
- The first few days of the microcycle are preferentially directed to conditional-coordinative structures whereas the last few days to coordinative-cognitive structures, always respecting the inter-systemic compromise between structures.
- The microcycle should respect an undulating load distribution, with a descending dynamic in the case of playing a difficult game at the end of the week. In the case that the team plays an easy game in the weekend, the load can show an increasing tendency during the microcycle.

Seirul·lo (2005b) uses an additional criterion to classify the sequences: disperse and concrete. Disperse sequences are those practiced with a higher frequency during all the season, as they contain variable elements which require the interaction of different systems. On the other hand, concrete sequences, less variable, are used sporadically during the year, as when coming back from an injury or to reach a certain level of shape.

After establishing the organisation strategies and the shaping sequences, the next step for the coach is to design preferential simulation situations (Seirul·lo, 2000). These situations are the training essence and represent what traditionally has been understood as "training tasks or exercises" (Seirul·lo, 2005b). The main difference between them is that preferential simulation situations are based on nonlinear behaviours, aiming to create an environment which determines a preferential action of any of the footballers systems towards the "differentiated self-shaping" (Seirul·lo, 2002). For instance, it is not just creating a deterministic task (e.g. jumping five hurdles in a straight line), but designing situations which facilitate a great level of interactions between the majority of the structures of the footballer (conditional, coordinative, cognitive, socio-affective, emotion-volitive, and so on). Seirul·lo (2002) establishes the following criterions to be respected when designing these preferential simulation situations:

- The tasks should require the participation of different systems which configure the hyper-complex structure of the footballer.

- Each player, according to his self-structuring level, will have a preferential use of certain systems to intervene in the playing scenario.
- When practice contains the required elements, new self-organisation levels can emerge.

The Structured Microcycle characteristic is achieved when preferential simulation situations configure a common scenario, keeping a relationship with the previous and posterior microcycle (Seirul·lo, 2005b). That is, each microcycle is not independent from the remaining ones and there is an underlying directional orientation in the process. By doing so, the footballers can maintain their sporting shape during a long competition period.

As the names suggests, preferential simulation situations should have a priority focus on each microcycle. From a practical point of view, this means that the coach has to select a preferential direction regarding a system and, from here on, training contents should be organised searching for an inter-systemic optimisation. This preferential direction will be different for each microcycle.

Seirul·lo (2005b) emphasises that the concatenation of preferential simulation situations must never be based on linear progressions. If done so, the footballer can experience performance decrements as they would block his optimisation process. Therefore, highly variable and dynamic situations have to be implemented, leading to system instabilities. When the footballer is taken to these open situations, he has to self-organise himself, relating all his structures and increasing the quality of his shaping process. It is essential to include these variable elements in training as Seirul·lo (in Cappa, 2007) explains:

> *All our training sessions at Barça are based on changes. We never do two identical training sessions, with the same intensity or the same objective. If we do so, on the third day the players will not work at their maximum. It would not be useful. Habits generate initial stability, but they end up destroying. The players, in order to adapt to the new training, have to use the energy they had parked and the team benefits from this... The players lose interest if there are too many repetitions. From the coaches I have had at*

> Barça, those who have better managed these aspects obtained better results.

Even the initial part of the training session should avoid the repetition of contents, as Seirul·lo replied in the year 2000 (Seirul·lo, 2000):

> I am convinced (there has not been a study on this) that if we are warming-up every day in the same way and the same time (same exercises and order), at the end of 10 days we will be colder than what we were at the beginning (physiologically speaking).

In addition, preferential simulation situations have to be organised to help the footballer understand the events of the game, identifying those elements which are in the same sphere as the style of play of the team. This is why Arjol (2012) gives credit to the participation of the player to define them, as when the player recognises them in training, the situations will be more significant for him.

One of the most characteristic training situations of FC Barcelona is the *rondo* (box) where players in the outside of a space pass the ball while one or two players in the inside work on its recovery. Cruyff (in Suárez, 2012) exemplifies the initial reluctances he found when applying this training content by saying, "I know many people laughed at the *rondos*, but the *rondo* is the base of football: speed, touch, short spaces..." The *rondo* is a classic visual image from training sessions at FC Barcelona but it can also be identified in their style of play, showing a great transference between training and competition. FC Barcelona Academy training methodology director, Joan Vila (2012), justified its utilisation by saying:

> The rondo has been in Barça since 1970s, although it was perfected by Cruyff. In rondos and positional games we have all the components that training must have: combinative playing speed, cognitive game features (with or without the ball), rational space occupation, individual and collective concepts and physical load control.

Preferential simulation situations at FC Barcelona are based on the previous foundations: position, movement, precision, possession, speed, etc. Hence, these situations must partially replicate some of the game characteristics, favouring the occurrence of expected behaviours without excessively reducing the intrinsic complexity of football (Cano, 2012).

First Team player Andrés Iniesta emphasises that, "Since then [when he joined FC Barcelona aged 12], everything has been with the ball, with the same training direction in the U12s, U16s or U19s. You change team but retain the game" (in Suárez, 2012). Again, Vila (2012) brings more light to this topic by saying:

> *There is never a specific physical work [in FC Barcelona´s training sessions], never. Only when the player is aged over 16 the ball games use wider spaces to develop power and endurance. When they are under 16 it is not necessary.*

One of the greatest footballers of the last decade, Xavi Hernández, praised this training conception by arguing the following in a newspaper interview (in Suárez, 2009):

> *This is Can Barça [FC Barcelona´s home]: rondos, infinite ball possessions... Joan Vila taught us these concepts. We do not do some of these drills in the First Team, as some players have not been grown up here. It is not the same a rondo with Iniesta or with me, even with Oleguer when he was here, that with the Brazilians, that stop the ball. I remember that Ronaldinho did not give the ball the same speed. With us, home grown players, you cannot see the ball. It's a marvel. Sometimes Rexach [former FC Barcelona´s assistant manager], who was with his back to us, shouted 'great, great!' 'You have not seen it' we said to him. 'I listen to the ball and I know it is going well', he replied. He knew it because of the touch, the noise.*

Figure II.9 shows one of the training situations which can be used to achieve a good positional play. This task is a traditional 7v7 ball possession game with three neutral players (in black). Most of the coaches would probably recognise themselves doing this kind of tasks, as they have probably used them in training.

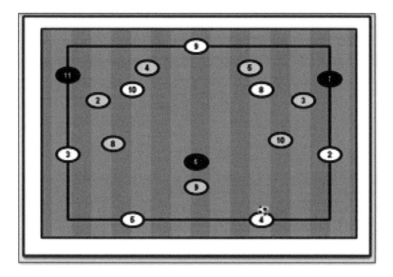

Figure II.9 An example of a preferential simulation situation: 7v7 ball possession game with three neutral players (in black).

If we look in detail at Figure II.9 we can better appreciate that the players are not positioned by chance in the space, as each of them has a selected area of influence. This way, when we look at Figure II.10 we can find the passing lines built between the players, identifying a playing matrix which is an essential characteristic of FC Barcelona´s style and playing formation (1-4-3-3).

Complex Football

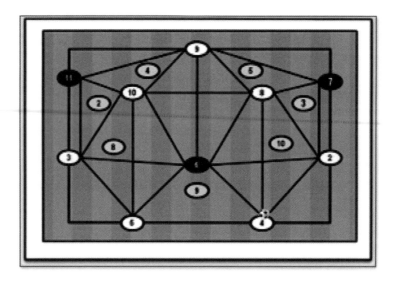

Figure II.10 Passing lines in a preferential simulation situation (7v7 ball possession game with three neutral players).

The playing philosophy of the team must be respected when designing the preferential simulation situations and can even show cultural differences with other styles of play. As an example, after being asked if English teams were fitter than FC Barcelona before taking part in the UEFA Champions League final from the year 2009, Seirul·lo replied (in Gómez, 2009):

> *Culturally, they [English teams] play direct football. It is more attractive because it is played on the penalty box. The transitions are quick and it seems as if there is a very high intensity, but that is tricky. Against Barça, English teams have been running after the ball; that is not playing football. Football is played with the ball. The one with the ball plays. The other one runs.*

This idea of training the game based on the game itself is characteristic of FC Barcelona and even top-class players, which have followed traditional models, can experience complications when they step into FC Barcelona's training ground. As an example, Lilian Thuram, World Cup winner in 1998 and runner-up in 2006, refers to this by saying in a recent interview (Morenilla, 2013):

> *When I was 34 years old and arrived at Barça, which was incredible for me as I was old, and saw how they were playing I asked myself: 'What was I doing before?' I thought it was the true game of football. Now, I can say that I can feel as a real football player after having played for FC Barcelona. It was a sin not having arrived younger, because with 34 I was very conditioned after 10 seasons in Italy. Especially for a defender, it was very difficult to change at that age.*

This different football conception was also highlighted by another World Cup winner, Gianluca Zambrotta, who ironically commented that when he signed for FC Barcelona he was always inside the *rondo* and even Victor Valdés, the goalkeeper, was better than him playing the ball with the feet (Domenech, 2013). Seydou Keita, international player for Mali, also reflected the difficulty of adaptation in the words of Vila (2012), "When he had been working one week at FC Barcelona he went to Guardiola´s office [at that time FC Barcelona´s manager] and told him, 'I can´t play this way! I don´t see the ball!' Vila (2012) also refers to Abidal, who showed a great humility and worked very hard during two or three months to integrate into the playing identity of the team. Lorenzo Buenaventura (in Perarnau, 2014) gives clues to understand why this happens:

> *Despite the age, there are many things in which you can improve. Technique is one of them. I have spoken about this many times with Paco Seirul·lo. The players who have arrived to Barça have many problems to adapt, because of its special methodology. I remember David Villa´s first training sessions. Even though he is a fast guy, dynamic and that he knew eight or nine players from the national team, it took him a long time to get the dynamic. The players have the capacity to improve the technique and the tactical sense despite being more than 30 years old; there is no doubt about this.*

As a summary to this section and in order to put the Structured Training process into practice, Seirul·lo (2005b) claims that organisation strategies (training programs in the classical textbooks), shaping sequences (training systems or methods) and preferential simulation situations (training tasks) must all be related, always respecting the complexity of the human being.

II.4.3 Design tasks in Structured Training

These tasks represent a short-term perspective of the training process. At the beginning of the season the coach elaborates a general view of what he thinks the season would look like, based on his knowledge and experience. These are the structural features of the season plan, with aprioristic graphs and representations similar to those shown from Figures II.4 to II.7. Once the season commences the coach must adjust all the processes on a daily basis, designing the most suitable training contents for the footballer and the team for each moment of the year, without leaving the general plan and being coherent with the project of the team. In this sense, Seirul·lo (in Díaz, 2011) explains that based on the initial principles "a general plan is developed. Additional questions are the day to day constraints, which take you to another plan, which, at the most, is on two weeks perspective." In the same interview, Seirul·lo refers to the peculiarities of planning the 2011-2012 season, where FC Barcelona had to perform at its best in uncommon stages of the season as in the Spanish Super Cup in August (as they had to play against Real Madrid) or in December (when taking part in the FIFA Club World Cup) by saying:

> *It will be a season with a similar general plan [as in the other seasons he had been in charge of the FC Barcelona first team], but with almost weekly modifications, small variations in specific things, things which we study depending on how the competition develops.*

The Structured Microcycle becomes relevant under this weekly interaction pattern. Seirul·lo (2005b) established five different kinds of Structured Microcycles, each of them with a different priority order in the way to organise the training contents in accordance with the objectives to be achieved. The characteristics of these weekly designs, which are also used by Roca (2009), are:

- **Preparatory Structured Microcycle:** Characteristic in the re-introduction to training after the transition period. It is principally formed by general and directed sessions, although even special sessions can be implemented. Generic sessions are not employed in this microcycle.
- **Directed Transformation Structured Microcycle:** It is a progression from the previous one with predominance of directed and special sessions.
- **Special Transformation Structured Microcycle:** Very closely related to the Directed Transformation, with a prevalence of special and directed sessions in this case.
- **Competitive Structured Microcycle:** In this weekly design special sessions and competition are the most relevant. This microcycle is a characteristic of weeks with two competitive games. Special contents are designed in one or two consecutive sessions, on two different days.
- **Maintenance Structured Microcycle:** This is the most characteristic design during the competitive period, with a similar presence of directed and special sessions and competition.

Once these five kinds of microcycles have been defined, the coach has to decide when to use them in the course of the season. Pre-season usually commences with Preparatory Structured Microcycles. The number of microcycles is dependent on the player characteristics. Top-class footballers normally have a very short transition period (four weeks) so they resume training with a good sporting shape. On the other hand, lower standard footballers coming from a longer off-season period might require two or three preparatory weeks.

From the second week of the pre-season on, Directed Transformation Structured Microcycles are used. As it was previously explained, footballers need to reach a high sporting shape as fast as possible, so generic and general workloads cannot be predominant in training during these first weeks. Special Transformation Structured Microcycles can also be employed in the second half of the preparatory period.

During the pre-season, Seirul·lo (2005b) organises three or four configuration levels for a certain structure, with a preferential orientation towards a system from this structure. As an example, the coach can select a structure (conditional) and a system from that structure (endurance) and design three configuration levels to be consecutively achieved during the microcycle, that is, in three days. On the first day more general contents could be employed, focusing on the preferential structure of the microcycle. Taking up the previous example again, training on the first day could be focused on the conditional structure and endurance system using general tasks. On the next two days, inter-systemic relationships with other structures could be searched by using preferential simulation situations. The design of the configuration levels and the distribution of general, directed and special contents has to be done in accordance with the requirements of each individual situation.

Competitive and Maintenance Structured Microcycles are characteristic of the competition period. Special Transformation Structured Microcycles are used in this stage of the season to take to or to maintain a high level of sporting shape. On the other hand, Directed Transformation Structured Microcycles can be used during moments with a lower density of competitive fixtures.

Only two configuration levels for a certain structure are proposed by Seirul·lo (2005b) to be used during the competitive season. With respect to Figures II.7 and II.11a, these two configuration levels can be organised on Tuesdays and Wednesdays when the matches are played on Saturdays. As the example of Figure II.11a shows, training contents in the Season Block (Tuesday and Wednesday morning) are related to two different systems (endurance and strength) from the same structure (conditional). All the alternatives have to be agreed by the coaching staff, so everybody is involved in their implementation, and can even be related to the next opposition team in competition. From a practical point of view, Roca (2009) shows the Structured Microcycle training load organisation in FC Barcelona´s first team in weeks with one (Figure II.11a) or two (Figure II.11b) competitive matches.

(a)	Mon	Tue	Wed	Thu	Fri	Sat	Sun
AM		Directed Endurance	Dir./Spe. Strength	Tec.-Tac. Tasks	Tec.-Tac. Tasks		Recovery or Day Off
PM	General Strength	Tec.-Tac. Tasks			Video Analysis	MATCH	

(b)	Mon	Tue	Wed	Thu	Fri	Sat	Sun
AM	General Strength	Tec.-Tac. Tasks		Recovery	Tec.-Tac. Tasks		Recovery or Day Off
PM			MATCH		Video Analysis	MATCH	

Figure II.11 FC Barcelona's Structured Microcycle when playing one (a) or two (b) competitive matches per week (after Roca, 2009).

At this point any reader might ask, when are the players going to the gym in Structured Training methodology? There is a constant debate in modern football regarding gym training and injury prevention strategies and Seirul·lo (in Cappa, 2007) argues:

There is an error: always assigning the responsibility for injuries to fitness conditioning. There are two things in football: accidents and injuries. Accidents, which are many, are unavoidable, and injuries, which are few are avoidable. It is an error using generic weights in movements and loads which are foreign to football. Weights prepare the muscle for other kind of activities which are not the ones that the footballer is going to use on grass. And this generates overuse injuries. Bodybuilding has to be used to improve strength focused on football, not generically. It is different if a 16-19 years old footballer needs muscle formation to transform him from an ordinary citizen to a sportsman. But it is best if this can be achieved with the ball. Why? Because using the ball adds the coordinative element that you are later going to use on the field. If you are doing three jumps without the ball, as an exer-

cise, it is nonsense. The place where you are jumping, your contacts... Everything is different when you have a ball in between. That is why you have to do it with the ball. It is not the same jumping than jumping to direct a pass. That is why physical preparation in football has to be done with the ball. The concept is mistaken. The question is not getting strength on the legs but adapting the muscles to what you are going to do on the field. The opposite generates injuries, as the muscle is not prepared.

Seirul·lo includes all these kind of contents in what he defines as "adjuvant training" (Seirul·lo, 1986). This type of training allows the footballer to take part in the optimising session. Thus, adjuvant training may precede optimising training and should be personalised for every player according to his individual necessities, as it can happen due to a player having sustained previous injuries. In other words, it can be used as a preparation for training and be focused on isolated structures (as the conditional structure), whereas the optimising training session must search for synergies between different structures (e.g. conditional, coordinative and cognitive).

II.4.4 Control and Evaluation tasks in Structured Training

The quantification of training workloads is necessary in any process. In order to do so in Structured Training, the quantitative representation of the weekly load can be obtained by the session frequency and the number of structures and systems which are involved. On the other hand, the qualitative components can be identified by how the shaping sequences and the preferential simulation situations are organised, to allow establishing dynamic interactions with the remaining microcycles (Seirul·lo, 2005b).

Complementarily, control tasks aim to verify the effectiveness of training contents on the person and, thus, models which are external to the footballer cannot be proposed (Seirul·lo, 2002). Seirul·lo (2005b) believes that this can be achieved by examining the systems performance in two training days, using capacities tests, biological examinations or by subjective assessments carried out by the player. In a more practical way, Seirul·lo emphasises that the way to control training has to go beyond the traditional laboratory tests as he reflected in an interview from the year 2001 (Seirul·lo, 2001):

> *Objective observations on certain key conditions from the training tasks must be employed for training control. These training tasks are those habitually carried out by certain group of players and have to be considered as extremely useful to recognise the optimisation level acquired in those systems that allow realisation to each player. No additional test is needed. ... It is difficult [for footballers to perform at their maximum in maximal laboratory tests], as they see it distant from their field practices. But this is not the only justification which makes this kind of test valid or invalid for training load design. If we are using general methods, these tests are useful, but if our proposal includes special methods, these tests are worthless, as they measure generic qualities. The same happens with different field tests. We should be coherent to know what we want a certain test to give us and not ask for what they cannot give us or what is even worse, mediate our practice because the test gives us a result whose interpretation confuses our decisions regarding the type of training we are going to do. Is it true that we cannot predict the performance of an engine in Daytona´s 24 hours just by analysing with the best audiometer in the world the idling speed noise?*

Evaluation tasks are used to know the effects in competition. The real goal of evaluation should be to detect the self-organisation level of the player, how he interprets his performances in each situation (Seirul·lo, 2002). In order to fulfil this aim, the coach has to develop his own evaluation strategies. The traditional approach to this process has been the collection of quantitative data, although Seirul·lo (2001) warns, "Quantifying reality this way means losing its context and de-contextualised data are not worthy for evaluating and decision making about an individual or a process." Therefore, Seirul·lo (2005b) encourages evaluating not only the result, but also the process. To do so it is important to use qualitative data, including subjective and objective evaluations, performance measurements and external judgements from competition.

©Miguel Ruíz/F.C.Barcelona

PART III

FRADE'S TACTICAL PERIODISATION

"Nobody has the necessity of all that unknown to him"

José Mourinho

III.1 VITOR FRADE: THE FATHER OF TACTICAL PERIODISATION

Does anyone know a football coach who does not consider himself a tactical expert? To be honest, most fitness coaches think their players are the fittest of the league. These affirmations are a consequence of the dissociative conception of football which was explained in the initial chapter of this book, where tactical and physical represented different dimensions of the player and the team. Therefore, under this philosophy, it is not surprising that when results in competition are not as expected the manager turns towards the fitness coach expressing his concerns, "The players are not fit enough", "All the other teams run more than us in the matches" or "We always look tired at the end of the games." The fitness coach, in a lower hierarchical position to the manager, avoids confrontation and habitually finds two solutions. First of all, he tests the players using a nonspecific running test to show he is not the cause of the problem, as the players are currently fitter than when they first did the test (how could they not be if this initial test was administrated on the first few days after coming back from the summer break!). In addition, he reinforces physical contents during the following sessions. Now, the players run more in training but arrive fatigued to the games, which increases the chances of losing the matches and sustaining injuries. Once this vicious loop has been installed, if the manager is unable to accurately identify the critical events that were related to the impairment of team performance, the coaching staff have all the chances of being sacked in a couple of weeks.

Tactical Periodisation questions the traditional reductionist conception of football. However, despite its increasing popularity, not many people really understand its foundations. As coaches are mainly concerned with tactics, it is not strange that many of them have quickly identified themselves as Tactical Periodisation users once they heard it was José Mourinho´s training methodology. Moreover, fitness coaches —who are normally in charge of periodising training workloads— were also attracted to this winning concept assuming that Tactical

Periodisation aimed at introducing the ball in the training drills. Altogether, many coaches (interested in tactics) and fitness coaches (in periodisation) have created their individual interpretation of Tactical Periodisation, in most of the cases with little to do with what it really means.

It is impossible to understand Tactical Periodisation without the figure of Professor Vítor Frade (Coimbra -Portugal-, 1944). All the biographical references available in the literature from this author reveal a singular character, away from conventional norms. As a pupil, he manifested a nonconformist approach to Classical Thinking which led him to academic experiences in different faculties such as engineering, sports sciences, philosophy or medicine, always looking for responses to the multiple questions that bombed his head. In parallel, he accumulated life-situations during his years as a professional football player and coach in different Portuguese teams, which combined with his restless character made him eager to learn about the sport.

The concept of Tactical Periodisation was developed around 30 years ago and, since then, has been subjected to all the influences received by Vítor Frade during the following decades (Tamarit, 2013). As the classical training methodologies did not provide conclusive answers to many of the football theoretical and practical dilemmas that had arisen during his teaching and coaching experiences, Vítor Frade searched for a new way to do things in football. Rui Faria (in Oliveira et al., 2007) emphasises the difficulty of this process as "to this day, changing the concepts and breaking with the norm is very difficult for many, daring for others and short-sighted for the majority." Therefore, Tactical Periodisation can be considered as a rebellion against the dogmatic training principles and its organisation, which have been universally expanded without being contrasted under the peculiar and specific football context.

Based on his knowledge, Vítor Frade highlighted the importance that the brain and the central nervous system had on motor activities, going beyond the traditional separation between body and mind. In this sense, he cemented his new vision of football in a diversity of sciences (neuroscience, complexity sciences, systems theory, chaos theory, topology, fractal geometry, cybernetics, psychology or anthropology) which helped him to combat the reminiscences of Classical Thinking in sports and to open an innovative and alternative conceptual framework in football. This implies that in Tactical Periodisation coaches not only require a great knowledge about football, but also about many other complementary areas, because "who only knows about football, does not even know about it" (Frade, in Tamarit, 2013).

Tavares (2013) defines Tactical Periodisation as "a football training methodology that conceives the training process as a teaching-learning process" and "has its own methodological principles that are different from other classical approaches." Its name is a consequence of the combination of two critical concepts: Tactical, as football prioritises decision making in a team specific context, and Periodisation, which refers to the temporal requirements to acquire the desired way to play (Oliveira, 2007). Tamarit (2007) reinforces the previous definitions as its "maximum concern is the type of playing that a team pretends to produce in competition." As it will be detailed in the following pages, Tactical Periodisation consists of a conceptual matrix (Playing Idea) conjugated to a training matrix (Methodological Principles), which are continuously interrelated and must be understood under a systemic perspective (Tamarit, 2013).

It was under the sport sciences environment, in the Faculty of Porto (Portugal), where Professor Frade reached the best platform to express this revolutionary training methodology, serving as a differential mentor for all the pupils that took his classes over the years. The theoretical knowledge developed by Professor Frade in this Faculty found FC Porto as a magnificent loudspeaker to spread the message. In the last few years (until June 2014), FC Porto has reached abundant success not only at Portuguese national level (winning 9 of the last 12 League championships) but also at European level (2003-04 Champions League and 2002-03 and 2011-12 UEFA Cup/Europa League winners). In this period two managers, José Mourinho and André Villas-Boas, have reached global relevance, both of them sharing a common identifiable feature: Tactical Periodisation. Mourinho publicly reinforced this idea by saying that the only difference between him and the other managers was the way he trained (Oliveira *et al.*, 2007).

From all of the above, it comes as no surprise that Porto has been located as an inexcusable pilgrimage place for all the coaches for whom the traditional approach to football training does not satisfy all personal concerns. The binomial between University of Porto and FC Porto has allowed establishing a link between theory and practice, being Vítor Frade the ideologist of this transgressive football training conception which handles the "unshakeable wholeness" of the game in order to achieve "Superior performance" (Tamarit, 2007, 2013).

©Real Madrid C.F.

III.2 THE GAME MODEL

Every football supporter enjoys a certain type of playing style, which can be defined with a great variety of elements: possession game where all the footballers take part in the action, direct play with long balls to the forwards, high pressing after losing the ball, dropping back and then counter-attacking as soon as recovering possession, etc. Many anthropological and sociological issues influence the way each of us understands the sport, which opens a wide range of possibilities on how people interpret and react during a match.

When people move from being spectators, mere external observers from the situation, to take a role as a coach of a football team, things dramatically change as this new responsibility demands a direct effect on the way a team plays. The coach is no longer foreign to the playing scenario and participates on its configuration, which requires seeing the game through a different prism to be able to captain the process. The initial mental representation that the coach has on his mind regarding how he wants a team to play is defined by Frade (in Tamarit, 2013) as the "Playing Idea."

The elaboration of the Playing Idea is the starting point of the process and is originated in the experiences and reflections from the coach, drawing the basics of what he wants the team to look like and achieve during the game, that is, an ideal representation of the kind of football he desires to build up (Oliveira, 2003). The coach has to try to be as precise as possible to clarify his playing conception, as the clearer and more coherent the picture is, the easier it will be to transmit it to the footballers and for them to understand it. This is essential, as ultimately, the players are in charge of putting the game organisation pretended by the coach into practice.

To be able to do so, the coach has to structure and systematise all the key elements that configure his particular vision of the style of play in relation to the four moments of the game: attack, defence, attack-defence transition and defence-attack transition (Pereira, in Miranda, 2009). In addition, all the basic patterns of these moments have to be identified, concreted and hierarchised in principles, sub-principles, sub-principles of the sub-principles (sub-sub-principles) and sub-sub-sub-principles (Oliveira, 2003; Silva, 2008). This conceptual matrix has to be respected from the beginning to the end of the season, as it is the skeleton of the football ideology of the coach (Tamarit, 2013).

From all of the above, the Playing Idea is a theoretical declaration of what, in terms of collective playing organisation, the team has to achieve. The notion of "Game Model (as a Previous Intention)" appears when these assumptions meet a specific context, that is, when the type of football that the coach has in his mind is put on concrete under a particular reality (Frade, in Tamarit, 2013). The distance between the ideas of the coach and the circumstances would be the same as between the concepts of Playing Idea and Game Model. The closer both notions are, the closer the coach will be to his desired collective intentional organisation (Carvalhal, in Tamarit, 2013; Tavares, 2013).

Frade (in Tamarit, 2013) believes the Game Model is "everything, as it is the Playing Idea plus the circumstances." Once the coach has defined his playing conception and inserts himself in a specific reality, it is when he moves into the sphere of the Game Model. The Model is the pathway to bring together all the individual tactical thoughts of the footballers, so they all perceive and solve a game situation in the same way. It is a platform where acting strategies must converge to avoid individual reactions which dissipate collective energy and effectiveness. According to Silva (2008), it should be a long-term dialogic process between the coach and the players to develop the game language, setting the values and principles to achieve logic in the game actions.

This notion supports one of the traditional statements of all coaches, who proclaim that they want their footballers to play as a team. However, there are many cases in which the consecution of this aim is not as evident as it might seem due to the discordant thoughts and acts of some players. As a popular saying puts it, if four horses are pulling from a cart, the cart will move at the speed of the slowest horse. Hence, the lack of a common tactical culture in a team is a major constraint which compromises adopting and understanding a Game Model and this makes achieving Superior performance impossible.

Mourinho (in Oliveira *et al.*, 2007) in the year 2002, explained:

> *The most important thing for a team is to have a certain model, certain principles and to know them and interpret them properly,*

regardless of the players that are being used. Essentially, that is what I call organisation of the game.

Going further, in another interview from the same year, after being asked by a journalist how his desired team would look be like answered (in Oliveira *et al.*, 2007), "It would be one where, at any given time, at any given situation, all the players think in the same way. This is my idea of team concept and it is only possible with time, hard-work and composure." Another Portuguese manager, Vítor Pereira (in Miranda, 2009) defines the Game Model as the "behavioural dynamic", that is, what he wants to recognise when he sees his team playing.

At this point, it is important to highlight that the Game Model does not mean the same as the playing formation or system of play of a team (e.g. 1-4-4-2, 1-4-3-3, 1-4-2-3-1), as the latter only represents the static structure of the team. Once the ball is in play and the footballers are moving, the functioning and identifying features of a Game Model must be manifested, showing collaboration networks between all the members of the squad and individual and collective referential patterns, always in the benefit of a qualitative team organisation (Villas Boas, in Sousa, 2009).

The Game Model is influenced by different factors which, following Oliveira *et al.* (2007) and Tamarit (2013), can be:

- **Football culture of a country:** Every nation has its peculiar characteristics which makes that what people expect to see when attending to a match in a southern European country can be very different to that expected in a northern European one. It is not the same being in charge of Brazil´s national team than Australia´s, so it is very important for the coach to know about the football culture of where he is going to work in, in order to develop a Game Model which is in accordance with the environment. Villas Boas (in Ribeiro & Viana, 2013) details this when referring to the problems he experienced when managing Chelsea FC, as he tried to implement a determined game pattern in a country with a different culture.

- **Culture and history of the club:** This factor is closely related to the previous one, as clubs like FC Porto, FC Barcelona or Ajax Amsterdam have a defined style and conceive a special game aesthetic which need to be respected.

- **Structure and aims of the club:** Inside a league competition, it is not the same being in charge of one of the top clubs than managing a club which has been recently promoted to the division and has a very small budget. The way to play is different in clubs looking for promotion than in those whose objective is to avoid relegation.

- **Playing Idea of the coach:** This reflects the particular vision that every coach has about the game and, ultimately, how to develop it during training. We can find coaches that are concerned on scoring more goals than the opponent and others worried on conceding less than their rivals (Mallo, 2013). This shows two divergent ways to approach the same reality. Martín Acero & Lago (2005a) use the concepts of initiative and expectative which go beyond having or not having ball possession. In this sense, a team can have the strategic initiative of the game being out of possession of the ball or, on the other hand, the team can be in possession but expectative to the game.

- **Structure or system of play of a team:** Player formations have undergone a considerable number of variations during the years evolving from the classical pyramidal system (1-2-3-5) characteristic of the First World Cup in 1930 (Tassara & Pila, 1986), to contemporary systems as 1-4-2-3-1, 1-4-3-3 or 1-4-4-2. Interestingly, Frade (in Tamarit, 2013) predicts that the next revolution in football should occur at structural level.

- **Player capabilities**: Represents the human resources which are available for the coach to apply the Game Model. The previous experiences of the players will also be very important, especially when the training direction is different from the conventional, as it happens with Tactical Periodisation. Older players are usually more reluctant to methodological changes on their training style.

- **Others**: Under this heading all additional sources of uncertainty which might influence the design of a Game Model can be included, as the moment of the season when the coach takes charge of the team, the calendar of competitions, the material resources, the medical staff, and so on.

According to Frade (in Tamarit, 2013), when the Game Model is practiced on the field of play during the training sessions and competitive matches, Previous Intentions are transformed into "Action Intentions." This is the time when plenty of interactions occur between the players, so the coach must be permanently on alert to detect and take advantage of the new directions that the Game Model can take. The emergent conducts which are resultant from the players and context interactions should not affect the game matrix —the initial collective references— but help the evolution of the model (Tamarit, 2007). For instance, a Game Model represents an open and dynamic complex system, acting as a loop which is never closed or finished and can be permanently subjected to new interactions and emergencies. Hence, the Game Model is always present and under construction orienting all the activities carried out during the training sessions to privilege a certain playing direction (Oliveira, in Silva, 2008).

To give a practical example of how all this information could be brought together we can use the hypothetical case of a coach who, before the start of a season, systemises his Playing Idea. Regarding the offensive moment, the coach structures the team in a 1-4-3-3 formation and sets as main principle of this moment keeping the possession of the ball using dynamic circulations and giving width to the play, to open the opposition team defensive lines and disorganise the defence. This general principle can be further detailed into sub-principles, indicating positional references. As an example, wingers can be positioned near the sidelines to give amplitude to the attack, looking to create 1v1 situations against the fullbacks of the other team and searching to cross the ball to the penalty box.

When the pre-season commences, the coach inserts himself in a specific football environment. After studying the characteristics of the players he has in the squad, he realises that the wingers do not have the ability to solve 1v1 situations as expected, which affects the Game Model (as a Previous Intention). The coach has to reflect about this and find alternatives (e.g. changing the wingers to play in the opposite side so, instead of looking for crosses, they cut infield onto their stronger foot when they face 1v1 duels against the other team´s fullbacks). Nevertheless, these positional changes of the players do not affect the playing matrix of the coach, the ideological foundations. After training a couple of months, the coach detects the emergency of a particular interaction between the left winger and the left fullback. This interaction allows creating effective 2v1 situations in the last third of the field. This represents the Game Model as an Action Intention. The permanent scrutiny which the Game Model is subjected to will allow prioritising these behaviours to favour team functioning.

The Game Model has to be clearly detailed and explained to the players so they are able to understand what the coach wants in every moment of the game and what they have to do to achieve the expected qualitative team organisation (Tamarit, 2007). To ease this process, as previously mentioned, the Game Principles (or Action Principles, in Silva, 2008) have to be systematised into principles, sub-principles, sub-sub-principles, and so on (Oliveira, 2003). The articulation and inter-relation of these conducts will allow manifesting the desired game organisation on a regular basis (Silva, 2008).

The principles are generic behaviours which are desired to be acquired to help understanding the game (Tamarit, 2007), at the same time as being intentional references to solve the game problems (Silva, 2008). In this sense, Oliveira (in Silva, 2008) expands this notion by specifying that these conducts have to be reflected in collective —team— and individual —player— terms. When moving into a deeper level of analysis, sub-principles and sub-sub-principles will represent specific behaviours which occur inside the previous levels (Tamarit, 2007). Even though principles and sub-principles might refer to one moment of the game, they should be always articulated to avoid losing sight of the wholeness of the game. The process that avoids compromising the entirety of football is described by Frade (in Tamarit, 2013) as "reducing without impoverishing."

Tavares (2013) sets a series of team scales in which to apply the Game Principles which depend on the number of players involved and, going from a greater to a lower number of participants, are: collective, inter-sectorial, sectorial, group and individual. These categories manifest different relationships between the footballers according to their playing positions (Oliveira, 2003). Collective behaviours are those which include all the players of the team, as when 11v0 offensive plays are practiced. A sector represents a playing line (e.g. defenders) and, therefore, a sectorial exercise will be that where players of the same line work together (e.g. line of back four practicing defensive zone movements), whereas inter-sectorial relates players from different lines (e.g. three midfielders and three attackers working on finishing). Additionally, a group is characterised by footballers from different lines who collaborate together (e.g. central midfielder, right wing and forward working on crossing and finishing). Finally, the individual scale includes situations where interactions with other teammates are not significant.

It is important to highlight that these Game Principles, which are behavioural references, should never be misunderstood with the Methodological Principles, which will be explained in the next section. The use of images, of the team itself or of teams that share similar Game Principles, can be used so the players get a more precise idea of what it is pretended from them (Pereira, in Tamarit, 2013).

However, as the following pages will show, field training is imperative to experience the desired way to play and to create "intentional interactions" (Frade, in Tamarit, 2013). In this sense, Faria (2002, in Silva, 2008) believes that training should aid the development of the Game Principles for each moment of the game. To be able to do so, training tasks should be specific and privilege the appearance of selected behaviours. The importance given to the immediacy, the actual moment, in what Frade (in Tavares, 2013) calls "right here and right now" contrasts with other methodological currents where the manager leads the team but does not have a meaningful presence in the day-to-day sessions. The role of the coach in Tactical Periodisation is totally different as he is the main director of the process, requiring an exquisite sensibility to detect and reflect about all the significant events that occur during training and matches, in order to enrich the quality and evolution of the Game Model. The training tasks are only potential learning situations and the coach must adequately intervene to favour the acquisition of determined objectives (Silva, 2008).

Figure III.1 represents a practical example of how the Game Principles of a football team could be organised in different organisation levels, providing a schematic view of how to fraction the way of playing. From the basic team formation or structure/s (those which are more keen to be used during the season; e.g. 1-4-3-3 or 1-4-2-3-1) the coach can elaborate a hierarchical articulation of the Game Principles for each moment of the game. To illustrate this we can select a game moment (e.g. defensive moment) and identify one large principle for this moment of play which us, as coaches, would like to achieve (e.g. high zone pressing). In order to be able to reach this generic principle we have to systematise and articulate specific sub-principles which could be:

(a) Positional balance to organise the defence.
(b) Close in on spaces as a team.
(c) Press the player with the ball.

Therefore, we have gone from defining a large and generic principle (what we want for our defensive moment) to detail certain behaviours inside this moment. These sub-principles can be further specified so the players can best understand what they have to do while they are defending. Continuing from the previous example, when pressing the opposition player with the ball (third sub-principle) we can establish the following sub-sub-principles:

(i) Orientate the play to areas where the ball can be more easily recovered.
(ii) Select the right moment to press and get the ball back.
(iii) Facilitate gaining control of the ball in a second action.
(iv) Avoid the opponent breaking our pressing line with one pass.

If necessary, we could include another division, sub-sub-sub-principles, if we wanted to give more detail to our model.

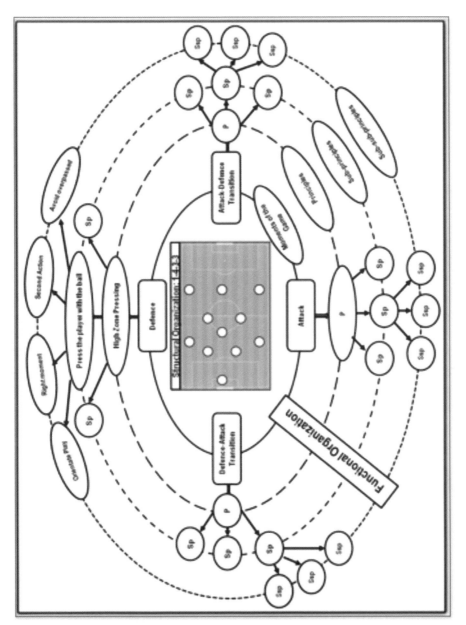

Figure III.1 Structural and functional organisation of a Game Model.

The previous is only a theoretical example of the way to do this process. However, as it is a very individual procedure, every coach should dedicate time to it, reflecting and systematising how he would like his team to look like and behave during competition. It is a singular and particular vision of the pretended way of play, setting collective and individual actions and behavioural references (Oliveira *et al.*, 2007).

Once the essential and characteristic features of the collective organisation have been determined (which represents the tactical dimension), the coach can further deepen into the situational aspects that arise when confronting a particular team in competition (the strategic dimension). The importance of the rival, the contextual environment, is never as important as the own team as Mourinho (in Oliveira *et al.*, 2007) precisely asserts:

> *We analyse the rival, we try to foresee how he is going to behave against us and, thus, we try to position in the most important areas of the field in relation to their strong and weak points. These are the position details. They do not interfere with our principles or our formation. We believe that we are the most important, the way we play and automate our model.*

When a coach is scouting a rival, what he is really doing is trying to determine the playing dynamics of a team, identifying the structural and functional behaviours which are repeated on a regular basis and characterised by the Game Model. This is represented by the principles of the collective and individual organisation of the players, which shows a selected pattern of behaviour (Oliveira, in Silva, 2008).

III.3 METHODOLOGICAL PRINCIPLES

As indicated in the previous section, the starting point for the coach is to define the Playing Idea he wants his team to reproduce. Once done so and taken into a context, the Game Model evolves without losing its identifying matrix, using the Game Principles to help the players understand and interiorise the organisation of the team. Training should put these hierarchised principles into practice in order to optimise "intentional interactions" between the players (Frade, in Tamarit, 2013).

The global playing conception reflects the concerns of the coach on the way to play football, so everything done during training should aid achieving this objective. It is surprising, however, the amount of time consumed by elite professional teams in nonspecific training contents which are far away from the sport: running in the forest, up-hill sprints, weight lifting, etc. Many of these coaches blame the lack of available training time when their team does not achieve success in competition.

This example serves to establish a critical difference between other traditional methodologies and Tactical Periodisation; in the latter case all the training process is directed to the tactical supra-dimension of the game (Tamarit, 2007). Mourinho (in Oliveira *et al.*, 2007) relates the anterior commandments by concluding that a coach should define his personal playing style and must always train in accordance with the game mode he pretends. This affirmation sets a bi-directional responsibility on coaches: conceptualising a Game Model and operationalising it during training (Tamarit, 2013). Thus, both realities have to be combined as the training methodology has to be, inexorably, subordinated to the Game Model (Oliveira *et al.*, 2007). Not all coaches are capable of accomplishing both duties, which can be an explanation for the existence of so many nonspecific contents during training sessions.

The only way that players experience and acquire the kind of playing that the coach desires is by respecting the ***Principle of Specificity***. This is an essential Tactical Periodisation principle which involves all the other ones and makes the process meaningful. Even if it does seem a rather trivial notion the number of times it is ignored is striking, as outlined in the previous paragraph.

For this reason, it has to be emphasised and placed above all the additional methodological guidelines as it will allow the footballers understanding the game, creating a tactical background and automating collective behaviours. By doing so, all the footballers should respond in the same way when they identify a common problem.

As its name suggests training in Specificity (in caps) reflects the necessity to map the behaviours which are desired to occur during the game. These kinds of conducts are adjusted to the conceptual hierarchy implemented by the Game Model and its corresponding principles. Based on this philosophy, the tactical dimension is prioritised over the other performance dimensions (physical, technical, psychological), which are always carried over and never considered as independent training aims (Tamarit, 2007). In this sense, Amieiro (in Tamarit, 2007) claims that "any technical or physical action always has an underlying tactical intention", as training is focused on assimilating a certain way of playing (Oliveira *et al.*, 2007).

As much as this might seem insufficient, training stimulus according to traditional reasoning, physical, technical or psychological dimensions evolve inside the Game Model without requiring additional exercises. In other words, the classical analytical conditioning or technical exercises have no relevance in Tactical Periodisation, as everything has to be directly related to the playing mode (Tamarit, 2007). Hence, contents as sprinting pulling a sledge and then shooting on goal, which are considered as specific training drills by some coaches, do not respect to Principle of Specificity, as these kinds of exercises have no effect to acquire the Game Principles or on the team organisation. In this regard, Frade (in Tamarit, 2007) highlights that "muscle contraction isolated from the Game Model Specificity of the coach will only limit the playing." Mourinho (in Oliveira *et al.*, 2007) brings more light to this topic by explaining:

> *When working on the tactical side in similar conditions to those we desire for competition and the kind of game we want, we are developing the physical side in Specificity. For example, instead of developing 'strength' in isolation or decontextualised, we are doing it through exercises with certain characteristics (playing with the space, time, number of players and rules). We are developing*

> *something related to 'strength', but in a more specific context. A tactical-technical exercise which at the same time contains lots of jumps, stops, changes of direction, is much more useful than developing strength in isolation. The difficulty of all this is to put what we want into practice, to implement adequate exercises that globe all sides, without forgetting our primary premise: to potentiate a determined game principle.*

The supra-principle of Specificity gives sense to all the process and becomes a "categorical imperative" (Frade, in Tamarit, 2013). Training exercises should help to experience the principles which shape the Game Model, helping to automatise the collective organisation (Oliveira et al., 2007). Rui Faria, in an interview from the year 2003 (in Oliveira et al., 2007) clarifies this by saying, "If the aim is to improve playing quality and organisation, those parameters can only be concreted through training situations or drills in which that organisation is required" and concludes that "training means improving the play." Furthermore, Mourinho is also keen on these aspects as he believes that the basis of the performance of a team is its playing organisation (Oliveira et al., 2007). Thus, everything done during training, even the warm-ups, should follow this reasoning and be focused on the way of play to be achieved (Pereira, in Tamarit, 2013). Hence, one of the main duties of the coach is "to find exercises that take the team to do what it is pretended during the game" (Mourinho, 2003, in Oliveira et al., 2007).

Tamarit (2013) indicates that, in addition to the relationship with the Game Model, in order for the exercises to be Specific they should have the following characteristics:

- The players must understand the objectives.
- The players need to maintain high levels of concentration.
- The coach should step in under selected circumstances, in accordance with the interactions revealed.

The necessity to train in concentration was previously highlighted, back in 1993, by other top-class managers such as Fabio Capello by saying (in Suárez, 2012), "The important thing is not training many hours, but doing it intensively and with a great concentration. You have to try to reproduce the stress situations of the game, because you will play they way you train." Training in (tactical) concentration reflects the ability to select important information from the environment during the entire training session or competition. This decisional concentration is also specific to the way of play and, in order to enhance it, Mourinho (in Tamarit, 2007) believes that requires complex drills where the players have to be permanently thinking and communicating, as it cannot be acquired just by using analytical exercises. In this sense, Mourinho explained the following in the year 2002 (in Oliveira *et al.*, 2007):

> *Like I always say, one of the things that makes training more intense —and when we talk about intensity we are [habitually] talking about energetic expenditure— is the required concentration. For example, running for the sake of running has a natural energetic expenditure, but its complexity is null and, for instance, its emotional expenditure tends to be null. The opposite occurs in complex situations where the players have technical, tactical, psychological and thinking requirements; this is what represents exercise complexity and drives to a greater concentration.*

In addition to the Principle of Specificity, there are three other Methodological Principles (the Principle of Propensities, the Principle of Complex Progression and the Principle of Horizontal Alternation in specificity) which are also needed to be respected. All of these principles are interdependent so they must be understood together as a unity, being correctly articulated to shape a holistic view of Tactical Periodisation. As it will be seen during the subsequent pages, these principles differ from those traditionally found in training theory and practice textbooks.

The ***Principle of Propensities*** highlights the necessity of designing training contexts which make it possible for certain behaviours to be manifested with a greater frequency. That is, training tasks which take the players to carry out a greater density of selected conducts. It is very important to clarify this point, as many times training is organised in the opposite direction. For example, under traditional reasoning, when a coach wants a player to do a certain action (e.g. shooting on goals) he creates an exercise which repeatedly solicits this action (e.g. line of players, drive the ball and shoot on goal from the edge of the penalty box). The perspective is different in Tactical Periodisation as the coach has to be worried on "giving birth to the contexts and not on the behaviours" (Frade, in Tamarit, 2013). This goes back to the axiom "reducing without impoverishing" from the same author. In addition, Tavares (2013) reinforces these ideas by saying that, "We coach large principles, sub-principles... not exercises or behaviours." For instance, if a coach wants his players to experience a high density of shooting he can design a 4v4 small-sided game which will probably lead to multiple finishing situations. Once the exercise is started, if he sees that the aim is not being fulfilled, he can modify the rules so that the principle needed to be manifested appears a greater number of times, in order words, "Condition the tasks so the pretended behaviour repeatedly occurs" (Tamarit, 2007). Rui Faria (in Campos, 2007) emphasises that it is critical for the coach to know exactly what he wants from the exercise, so when the players are practicing they are experiencing and living what the coach pretends.

The appropriate organisation of the training tasks helps the players to acquire the Game Principles (Tamarit, 2013). Maciel (in Tamarit, 2013) reinforces this by saying that these training contexts should lead to a dominance of the characteristic interactions of our style of play. The exercise modelling guarantees systematic repetition, which is crucial in learning activities and is the way to consolidate the principles of the Game Model (Oliveira *et al.*, 2007; Tamarit, 2013). In the year 2001, Mourinho (in Oliveira *et al.*, 2007) pointed out his training characteristics regarding this aspect:

> *We automate players with work and less daily fun. I think there are players in this country [Portugal] who have more fun than ours, who have fun training, but do not do it in such a methodical or demanding way. For us, each training day is a day with an important tactical content. There are things which have to be worked on, which require concentration and from which dividends are obtained... I do not trust playing formations originated in a cabinet, in a meeting, talking with the players. I believe in training, in explaining, in systematic repetition, in systematisation...*

Developing habits is essential in sports as it speeds up the decision making process (Tamarit, 2007). When a player is familiarised with certain game situations his tactical response will be faster, as the decision will be governed by the unconscious plane of the brain. On the other hand, if the situation is unknown, it would take the footballer a longer time to produce a response as the conscious plane of the brain will command the reaction (Tamarit, 2007). McCronc (in Silva, 2008) determines that the actions which require the participation of the conscious part of the brain take half a second. Under game constraints, it is essential to produce immediate effective responses to solve game related problems. Thus, when a player identifies a situation during competition that he had already experienced in training, he can anticipate the solution and take advantage from it (Faria, in Campos, 2007). The systematic repetition of the Game Principles enables the development of habits, anticipation mechanisms and consolidating the pretended way of playing (Oliveira *et al.*, 2007). In this regard, it is important that the basic principles and sub-principles of the playing matrix are repeated every week to keep them alive, as the players forget them if they are not continuously remembered (Tamarit, 2007).

From all of the above, it is crucial for the coach to create a guided learning process (Ruiz Pérez, 1994) so players perceive, think and experience different football specific situations which help to enhance their qualitative development. This intentional process will allow the players moving from the sphere of "knowing to do" to "knowing about knowing to do" (Frade, in Tamarit, 2013). Again, Frade (in Tamarit, 2013) gives this learning direction a key importance as during "learning-by-reception" the frontal cortex (rational part) of the brain is stimulated, whereas when "learning-by-discovery" the brain stem (which links actions to emotions) is activated. These emotions and somatic markers have been documented in different neuroscience studies (Damasio, 1996; Punset, 2010) to play a critical role in the teaching and learning process, as they form part of perceptions, decision making, reasoning, learning or memorising processes (Oliveira *et al.*, 2007) so we cannot conceive reason and emotion in different planes (Damasio, 1996).

The **Principle of Complex Progression** refers to the necessity of variation in the stimulus which the players are subjected to in the course of long and short term training cycles. The notion of complexity was explained in detail in the section I.2 of this book, representing a holistic approach to the process and not being just conceived as the difficulty or complication of a certain event (Morin, 1994). Faria (in Tamarit, 2007) clarifies this term and its application to a football context by defining it as "behavioural actions from a determined way of play." In addition, the notion of progression reinforces how the complexity of the situations planned during training should be alternated during the season to reach an adequate learning and teaching process which, ultimately, will lead the players to acquire the principles of the Game Model pretended by the coach. This progression can be achieved by ordering these Game Principles in accordance with their importance, avoiding interferences between them (Gaiteiro, 2006, in Tamarit, 2007). Progression must be related to conceiving training as a complex system, which configures a nonlinear process to enhance the quality of the way of playing (Tamarit, 2013).

As it was mentioned above, progression can appear at two different but inter-related levels: during the season (long term) or during the week and training session (short term). With a season long perspective, the first few weeks of the season should be dedicated to the hierarchical organisation of the principles and sub-principles of play in each of the four moments of the game. At the beginning, generic and less complex principles would be introduced in training and, once the players assimilate them, specific and more complex principles could be included. There is not a standard progression for all the teams as it would be dependent on the experience, capabilities and habits of the players (Tamarit, 2013).

On a short term basis, complexity has to be arranged in the weekly plan and in the daily session. This process requires having a detailed classification of the Game Principles, which will allow their appropriate sequencing and articulation during training. To be able to do so, Tamarit (2013) believes that it is essential to respect a correct relationship between effort and emotional recovery in the exercises. In addition, this author identifies the following characteristics to be considered when examining the complexity of an exercise:

- Articulation of the principles and sub-principles.
- Effort sub-dynamics and preferential muscular contraction pattern.
- Playing space.

- Exercise duration.
- Number of players involved.

The organisation of complexity progressions in the course of the week is closely related to the ***Principle of Horizontal Alternation in specificity***. In a very similar manner to what was previously reported by Tamarit (2013), Maciel (in Tamarit, 2013) explains that the key characteristics to organise the weekly plan should be:

(a) The level of complexity of the principles, sub-principles and sub-sub-principles.

(b) The dominant muscle contraction regimen (tension, duration and velocity).

(c) The strategic dimension, which would be dependent on the number of days between two matches, to allow emotional and effort recovery.

Frade (in Tamarit, 2007) precisely summarises this Principle in "training in Specificity without being in the same level of Specificity." Therefore, the playing of a team is disassembled in the course of the week, to facilitate a specific reintegration and building up towards the next competitive match. This guarantees that different levels of organisation are solicited every day of the week, ensuring an optimal regeneration without overloading the same structures (Tamarit, 2007; Silva, 2008). By consecutively doing so in a regular weekly pattern, the Morphocycle is developed. This training organisation will be explained in detail in the next section as it is another critical element which characterises Tactical Periodisation.

III.4 THE MORPHOCYCLE

In contrast to other training methodologies, the main planning unit in Tactical Periodisation is the Morphocycle. Etymologically, the root of this word (morph-) comes from the Greek μορφ-, which could be translated as shape. Additionally, in this specific context cycle represents the time between two successive competitive matches, which for the great majority of football teams would be around seven days long. Frade (in Tamarit, 2013) reinforces the importance of this concept as "the logic of Tactical Periodisation is based on creating a Morphocycle, which is underpinned by the Methodological Principles and enables operationalising the way of play."

The consecutive repetition of this planning structure aims to stabilise the performance of the team during the season, which is specifically manifested by the way of playing. This is another critical difference with other philosophies as Tactical Periodisation does not search for playing oscillations, which is, peaking in selected moments of the season. Rui Faria (in Oliveira *et al.*, 2007) clearly discusses this idea in an interview from the year 2003:

> *The existence of peaking is, in our opinion, associated to a different way to train from ours. Peaking is characteristic of sport disciplines which require long preparation periods and a short competition period. In football, with a 10 months long competition period and a 1-1½ month long preparation period, this peak is not important. What is convenient is maintaining maximal profitability during the competition period, without big oscillations.*

From the above, Mourinho (in Oliveira *et al.*, 2007) believes that the best indicator of the sporting shape is manifesting team organisation on a regular basis. To be able to achieve this optimal playing stability it is necessary to create a weekly training pattern —Morphocycle—, which is repeated from the beginning to the end of the season (Tamarit, 2013). Maciel (in Tamarit, 2013) goes further by saying that it does not only allow the stabilisation of a certain kind of playing but its progression, as new interactions emerge which facilitate the evolution of the Game Model. The dynamic structure of the weekly cycles is based on the management of the number and duration of training units, contents and recovery regimens (Oliveira *et al.*, 2007).

The workload distribution during the Morphocycle represents another fundamental difference with conventional training strategies. Volume and intensity parameters play a different role in Tactical Periodisation, with volume losing its traditional priority in the early stages of the season. Under this training conception, maximal relative intensities are requested since the first day as Mourinho (in Oliveira *et al.*, 2007) explains:

> *The common idea that volume and intensity differ between preseason and competitive season exists. There is talk about the necessity of starting with elevated working volumes, though with low intensities and later, as the competition approaches, invert this logic. All of this is seen under a physical point of view. I do not believe in this. For me, both periods are all the same. What I understand by intensity completely differs from the traditionally attributed meaning. I cannot separate intensity from concentration. When I say that football requires elevated intensities, I say it respecting its complexity and the permanent requirement of concentration which is needed. It is based on the principle that, for sure, the best way to recover from the holidays´ losses is working with maximal relative intensities associated to our playing characteristics. For that reason, I do not believe in volume increases and in the volume for intensity inversion. For example, what is normally called aerobic endurance, which is conventionally said to be acquired by training volume, can also be achieved with the accumulation of maximal relative intensities.*

This configures a different logic, as intensity is considered in Tactical Periodisation as "concentration intensity" and volume as "volume of concentration intensities", "volume of maximal relative intensities" or "volume of Game Principles" (Oliveira *et al.*, 2007). For this reason, training volume will remain the same from the second to the last week of the season, the differences being due to the increase of the intensity times and the reduction of the recovery intervals as the season progresses (Tamarit, 2007).

Based on this, Castelo (2001, in Tamarit, 2007) suggests that training sessions should not be more than 90 minutes long —including the pauses between drills— with only one session per day, to allow the players to recover for the next training day. Mourinho (in Oliveira *et al.*, 2007) coincides with this training duration and believes that the coach should be concerned in creating dynamic sessions characterised by fast transitions between exercises. These transitions should be used for active recovery in order to maximise uptime. Lengthening training duration will derive in the reduction of quality as the players will have problems to maintain the concentration demanded.

An additional feature of Tactical Periodisation in relation to conventional training approaches is the different notion of fatigue. Due to the Specificity of the process, physical and mental fatigue cannot be understood in different planes (Tamarit, 2007). Training in concentration requires greater mental and emotional demands on the players that what they are normally habituated to, leading to the development of "tactical fatigue" (Oliveira *et al.*, 2007). Mourinho (in Oliveira *et al.*, 2007) coincides with this by saying:

> *The most relevant fatigue in football is the central and not the physical fatigue. Any professional team minimally trained can resist a game, with more or less difficulty, from an energetic point of view. Central fatigue results from the capacity of being focused and, for this reason, all the players have to react immediately and in a coordinated way in the moment the ball possession is lost.*

Complementarily, Tactical Periodisation does not use the traditional physical capacities nomenclature (strength, endurance and speed) and focuses on the type of muscular contraction which is predominant. In this regard, muscular activations can show a preferential direction according to the tension, duration and velocity of the contraction. It has to be clarified that all of these components are always present in muscle contractions, but each of them can be privileged by the way the exercise or session is configured.

When all of this is taken together, a different operational logic to configure training organisation is developed. As Tamarit (2013) summarises, "Concreting the Game Model (as a Previous Intention) through the Methodological Principles is what allows Specificity to emerge and this is only achieved with the Morphocycle weekly presentation."

III.4.1 The first week of the season

This first week of the season can show some minor differences with the standard Morphocycle and for this reason the essential characteristics will be addressed in this section. As it was previously explained, the logic of Tactical Periodisation is different from conventional methodologies where physical components and accumulating training volume were the priority objectives during the initial days. Hence, from the beginning everything done in Tactical Periodisation has to be based on modelling the way of play and the training style which will be characteristic of all the season. Therefore, the Principle of Specificity governs the training direction since the commencement of the process.

These initial days have to be used by the coach to explain the essential features of the Playing Idea he has on his mind, trying to transmit to the players the identifying elements of the Game Model (as a Previous Intention). In order to help this process, the coach can use visual images with the aim that all the individual understandings converge in a common meeting point (Faria, in Campos, 2007). Tamarit (2013) clarifies this topic by saying, "What we pretend is to create a mental image of the play we want to acquire and little by little embody it, that is, allowing the mental image to arise with associated emotion in our players."

As all the Game Principles have been previously hierarchised the coach has to focus in this early stage on the large principles, respecting the Principle of Complex Progression. The game is dissembled to allow the players understand the situations and why everything is done, which will help them to acquire the conceptual matrix of the team (Carvalhal, in Tamarit, 2013). It is very important to make the players active participants of this learning process as "only the intentional act is educative" (Frade, in Tamarit, 2013).

Mourinho (in Oliveira *et al.*, 2007) feels that in this first week he wants the players to adapt to the game specificity and describes one of his previous pre-season coaching experiences in the following way, "The first four working days served for the re-adaptation of the players to the effort and, from there on, we started working as always, with maximal intensities." In addition, all the Methodological Principles have to be respected to create a similar training and competition pattern as the remaining weeks of the season. Frade (in Tamarit, 2013) reinforces this when he states "the human being is an animal of habits, so he needs to adapt to the Morphocycle from the first week."

After Oliveira *et al.* (2007) and Tamarit (2007, 2013), the aims of this initial week of the season can be summarised in:

- Presenting the Game Model (as a Previous Intention) to the players so they can create a mental image and embody it.
- Conceptual adaptation to tactical thinking (concentration intensity) and to the training logic.
- Developing affective and emotional relationships; players knowing each other and establishing common links.
- Gradual physical and physiological adaptation to the Game Model: motor patterns, energetic demands, effort:recovery ratios, etc. specific to the way of play.

III.4.2 The Morphocycle (from the second week of the season on)

The great majority of football training plans described to date have been only based on the physical side of performance. As it has been highlighted in different parts of this book, the holistic conception of the footballer and football rejects the isolated treatment of dimensions and emphasises the importance that mental-emotional components have on performance. Thus, body and mind, muscle and brain, cannot be considered independently from each other in the training process. As Castelo (in Tamarit, 2007) says, "Educating is not only about developing the muscles, but habituating the brain to command the body." Therefore, it is the responsibility of the coach to guide training to favour a certain direction in the right moments of the week, respecting the Principle of Horizontal Alternation in specificity.

As discussed earlier, the Morphocycle structure is introduced as early as possible at the beginning of the season, to ensure an adaptation to the playing way and to its metabolic demands, at the same time as looking for stabilisation through the development of habits. This process can even be started in the second week of the pre-season, after the first re-adaptation days when resuming training after the holiday break. Under the perspective of Tactical Periodisation pre-season is not conceived in the same manner as it has traditionally been done so, as the aim is to create a training structure which is going to be followed all the remaining weeks of the season (Frade, in Tamarit, 2013). For this reason, there are no great differences between pre-season and the competitive period in this training methodology, as Mourinho (in Oliveira *et al.*, 2007) details:

> ...*From the second weekly microcycle of the season on, and I am talking about the period which we conventionally call pre-competitive period, the microcycles are basically the same until the end of the season, both at the level of principles and working aims and at physical level. I only potentiate modifications on the elements at tactical-technical dominance level, in relation to the difficulties experienced in the previous game and analysing the next one... From the second week on, there are repeated weekly cycles. For instance, I only use weekly cycles. My 'main features' regarding the physical weekly pattern are the same in the month of July as in April of the following year.*

The interaction between training and competition is crucial, as training allows developing the kind of play we want the team to achieve in competition, at the same time that competitive games feedback what we need to do during training (Oliveira, in Silva, 2008). This configures a peculiar strategic dimension to operationalise the Morphocycle. The weekly plan cannot be isolated from the environment: where the team is coming from (the last competitive match) and where is he going to (the next match). That is why these two inexorable references are a constant feedback and feedforward to the strategy. The traditional aprioristic recipes, where the coach knows in advance what he is going to do in the subsequent weeks and months is inconceivable in Tactical Periodisation, as it is an open and dynamic system continuously subjected to interactions from the environment. This makes that long term plans are careless in this methodology, as everything has to be thought and developed on a day-to-day basis. Additionally, those fitness coaches that intervene in the training sessions but do not attend the competition games or do not holistically evaluate team performance in competition are clueless about the specific necessities that the team demands.

The Morphocycle is repeated during the season and is dependent on the number of official matches per week the team is involved in. In this sense, the most typical case would be that where a team plays a match every Sunday and, hence, the Morphocycle duration would be seven days long: from Monday to Sunday. By the same token, if a team regularly plays the matches on Saturdays, the Morphocycle would be from Sunday to Saturday. From this situation on, we can find particular situations which would need different considerations. As an example, teams playing two official matches per week, as those taking part in a domestic tournament on the weekends and in an international competition on midweek, will follow an adapted training organisation structure, the Exceptional Morphocycle, which will be explained in section III.4.3.

Taking into consideration one of the most common scenario, a team playing its competitive matches from Sunday to Sunday, the main objective of the first 48 hours after the match will be to ensure an appropriate recovery of the footballers. The central part of the week —Wednesday, Thursday and Friday— will form the acquisitive phase, whereas the last training day of the week —Saturday— has to ensure recovery from the previous days at the same time as preparing the team for competition on Sunday (Figure III.2). Following Oliveira *et al.* (2007) and Tamarit (2007, 2013), the organisation and objectives of the seven days Morphocycle shall be made respecting the considerations addressed in the following pages.

Sun	Mon	Tue	Wed	Thu	Fri	Sat	Sun
MATCH	DAY OFF	ACTIVE REC.	ACQUISTIVE PHASE			REC. + ACT.	**MATCH**

Figure III.2 The Morphocycle (after Oliveira et al., 2007; Tamarit, 2007, 2013). REC: Recovery; ACT: Activation.

Day 0 – Sunday: Competition

The competition match is the link between two consecutive Morphocycles. On the one hand, it is used to evaluate team performance and the effects of the previous training sessions. On the other hand, it paints the landscape which is going to contextualise the following week. This day belongs to the previous Morphocycle, but is should be kept as a reference to understand the distribution of the training contents during the subsequent days.

Day 1 – Monday: Day Off

After playing a competitive match on Sunday, the players are given the day off on Monday. This is not a universal rule for all circumstances, as there are times where logistic issues come before the desires of the coach. Having the day off after the most intense exercise of the week (the match) is a declaration of intentions of this training methodology. Again, this shows a different conception to conventional training rules as it is nowadays frequent for football teams to carry out a recovery session the day after a match and have the next day off (48 h after the game). Varied scientific studies based on the conventional paradigm have shown that certain physiological and biochemical markers present a better recovery if training is carried out in the 24 hours after a match (Ascensão et al., 2011; Baldari et al., 2004; Kinugasa & Kilding, 2009). That is why the foundation of teams training the day after a match is principally based on a physical perspective.

These kinds of studies reinforce the traditional dissociation between physical and mental-emotional fatigue. However, the mind occupies a central place in the logic of Tactical Periodisation so recovery needs to be holistically considered, including not only the physical, but also the mental and emotional fields of the sportsmen (and of the coach). After a competition fixture, the player is physically and, most importantly, mentally fatigued. If the match has had additional sources of stress as a tight score, crowd, pressure, etc. the emotional components would have been highly demanded. Under these circumstances, with an elevated hormonal production, it is very difficult for the players to go to sleep peacefully after a match. Mourinho (in Oliveira *et al.*, 2007) clearly explains his point of view about this topic:

> *When there is only one match in the week the players have the day off after the game. I know that it has been said that this is not the most appropriate from a physiological point of view, but it is from a mental point of view. And it also is for me as I do not like working the day after a match. It is hard for me to sleep after the game, it is hard to get up, it is hard to focus, it is hard to plan out, it is hard to think, it is hard to practice and, in those sessions, I spend more time walking back and forth than training. The same happens for the players. Anyone who thinks differently is fooling himself. From a physiological point of view it is better training the next day, although players do not like it, they do not feel well. It is best for the body, but worse for the mind. And we have to look at this matter from a global point of view!*

Former FC Porto manager Vítor Pereira fully agrees with the previous affirmations (Tamarit, 2013). For this reason, to facilitate mental-emotional recovery, the first 24 hours after the match the players are given the day off, resuming training on Tuesday.

Day 2 – Tuesday: Active Recovery

It is common sense that this day (36-48 hours after competition) players will not be completely recovered from the previous match. This makes that training components on this day have to be carefully selected to avoid increasing the risk of injuries and respecting that the main objective is to ensure an adequate active recovery from the precedent match. For this reason, this day has to safeguard the recovery process adding a Specificity connotation, which implies "training contents must be the same... experiencing [the principles, sub-principles, and so on] without dynamic" (Frade, in Tamarit, 2007).

The context to facilitate recovery has to include characteristics of the Game Model, being specific to the pattern of play and action. Therefore, Tuesday can introduce the players to the weekly training structure, starting the build-up using more generic and less complex principles and sub-principles related to the previous and following match, which can include situations without opposition or something not very difficult (Oliveira, in Silva, 2008). Pereira (in Tamarit, 2013) reveals an interesting appreciation in this regard, as during his practical experience detected that players had trouble concentrating on this day at certain stages of the season, manifesting "tactical fatigue." To combat this, he organised training in a more fun-oriented way on Tuesdays. By doing so, the mental demands of the tasks are reduced, aiding to recover the nervous system and the game related decision making capacity, which is essential for Specificity (Silva, 2008).

The exercise duration on Tuesday has to be very fragmented, with long recovery times and with a reduction in the tension, duration and velocity solicitations during muscular contractions (Tamarit, 2007). In a more recent publication, Tamarit (2013) explains that muscle contraction on this day should be characterised by a high tension, a high velocity, but with a very short duration, that is, with a very low density, just brief instants of tension.

Frade (in Tamarit, 2013) believes that in order to improve recovery processes, the energetic pathways have to be stimulated in a similar way than during competition. Thus, if competition demands a specific biochemical response — characterised by a mixture of aerobic, lactic anaerobic and alactic anaerobic metabolisms—, recovery cannot be achieved by only stimulating one of these pathways, as it has been habitually approached in football teams where players run at low speeds around the field.

Carvahal (in Silva, 2008) and Frade (in Tamarit, 2013) reinforce the idea of recovering in Specificity, with players needing to carry out a similar effort pattern as during competition, but with a smaller dose and much longer pauses in between, decreasing space, time and concentration requirements on the exercises. This way, the metabolisms are specifically solicited and recovery is optimised.

As it was previously pointed out, from a strategic point of view, training contents on Tuesday should be linked to what happened in the last competitive match: score, travel, playing surface, traumatisms, additional sources of stress, etc. and, specially, minutes played by each footballer. This is critical as training should not be the same for those players who completed 90 minutes in the precedent match than for those who played little or were even out of the squad. These players with lower match-play exposure must include training contents similar to competition on this day, although in a smaller dose.

Day 3 – Wednesday: Sub-principles and sub-sub-principles with a dominance of Tension in the muscle contraction

The main objective of the first 48 hours after the match was to ensure the recovery of the footballers, whereas from the third day on, the aim is to operationalise and acquire certain characteristics of the playing style. These situations present higher emotional demands on the players in relation to the previous day, as training activities have a greater similarity with the collective dynamics and the playing organisation (Silva, 2008). However, as three days after the match the players are not fully recovered yet, especially from an emotional point of view (Mourinho, in Oliveira *et al.*, 2007), training components should be adapted to the state of mind of the footballers.

Due to the Game Model being dissembled during the Morphocycle, the priority on Wednesday is focused on sub-principles and sub-sub-principles of the way of play, which represent a lower complexity of the situations. These principles are developed under inter-sectorial, sectorial and individual relationship levels, representing an intermediate fraction of the playing (Silva, 2008). The effort dynamic of the exercises should be characterised by high tension, short duration and an important velocity in the muscle contractions. Therefore, tension should be the muscular dominance of the training practices, achieving this by the presence of an elevated number of eccentric contractions, as it happens during acceleration, decelerations, changes of direction, jumps or shooting on goals.

The way to guarantee this predominant contractile pattern is by designing tasks based on small spaces, with short durations and involving a low number of players, so the overall density of tense muscular contractions is high (Tamarit, 2007). These constraints will allow the players exercising at their maximal relative intensities, as long as there are enough recovery periods between sets and drills. Frade (in Tamarit, 2013) believes that when practices are organised involving discontinuous efforts, the alactic anaerobic pathway becomes the predominant metabolism, as the long pauses between efforts would aid the recovery processes. The management of work and recovery ratios is essential; if exercising periods are too long or pauses excessively short, training effects can vary leading to the accumulation of lactate, with its subsequent limitations in performance (Frade, in Tamarit, 2013).

Due to its fractionation, Wednesday session can be the longest of the week. For instance, in selected moments of the season, especially at the beginning as the players might have trouble to maintain maximal relative intensities during the tasks, the coach can divide this session into two: a morning and an afternoon session. Frade (in Tamarit, 2013) stresses that doing this does not mean training twice as much, but splitting the session into two parts, to ease recovery and adaptation.

At this point, it is important to highlight that achieving a characteristic muscular contraction in isolation must not be the guide when planning the exercises, as the actions must be integrated into the articulation of sub-principles and sub-sub-principles of the Game Model of the team. Probably this has led to confusion in many papers and presentations about this Tactical Periodisation, from which people have understood that Wednesday is the day solely devoted to tension and coaches have created exercises which demand eccentric contractions on the players, away from the Specificity of the Game Model. Likewise,

Frade (in Tamarit, 2013) shows his concern with the way tension has been matched to strength, duration to endurance and velocity to speed, as if every training day presented the aim of developing a physical capacity in isolation. This is far away from the logic of Tactical Periodisation, where everything has to be related to the way the team wants to play, always searching for "intentional interactions" (Frade, in Tamarit, 2013).

Day 4 – Thursday: Large principles and sub-principles with a dominance of Duration in the muscle contraction

This is the central day of the week and players should be fully recovered from the previous match, as this was more than 72 hours ago. However, from a regeneration and strategic point of view, the next match must now be in the horizon and needs to be taken into consideration. The training configuration of this day should partially replicate the demands of competition, without this meaning playing a full pitch 11v11 game. This session presents the highest complexity of the Morphocycle as tactical attention is paid on the large principles and the sub-principles of the collective organisation, affecting the four moments of the game. The articulation of all the macro-principles is carried out at collective scale, involving all, or almost all, the players of the team (Oliveira, in Silva, 2008). Experiencing and acquiring these greater principles would lead the players to a high mental-emotional fatigue, though never as elevated as the demands of the official competition. As mentioned, the strategic dimension should be respected according to the characteristics of the next team to play against during the weekend.

Muscular contractions on this day must show a great similitude to competition demands, with predominance of duration and with tension and velocity slightly reduced in relation to the previous day (Oliveira, in Silva, 2008). As the game dynamic is unpredictable, it is impossible to ensure an absolute precision about how the contractions are going to occur during a training task; nevertheless, a determined direction must be privileged to safeguard the Principle of Propensities.

Training tasks on Thursday should be based on big spaces, longer durations and with the participation of a greater number of players, to allow collective interactions. As the effort dynamic is similar to competition, it will be the most continuous day of the week. However, the adequate use of pauses will aid the players to exercise at maximal relative intensities. Thus, for this purpose, it is better to carry out four sets of 10 minutes of a certain task rather than two sets of 20 minutes (Frade, in Tamarit, 2013). Dividing the overall exercise duration into smaller parts helps footballers to maintain higher concentration intensities. Recovery time between exercise bouts must allow the players to be fresh and spontaneous in the next set (Oliveira *et al.*, 2007). Altogether, this is the most demanding training session of the week as it involves a greater mobilisation of the organic structure (Maciel, in Tamarit, 2013). Mourinho (in Oliveira *et al.*, 2007) clarifies his vision on how this day should look like by explaining:

> *Training on Thursday is developed in wide spaces, with more movement, which approaches to what I call 'specific endurance', although it has nothing to do with the traditional idea of endurance. I do not do endurance training! In my opinion, endurance is adapting to a playing concept, it is being able to do collective and individual actions implied in our playing way. The only thing we do is train what we are doing in a game, in wide spaces and similar to real situations. Our concern is finding tactical contexts, playing situations, which allow a specific adaptation to our way of play. What I do not do is using all the space of the field, but that has to do with propensity contexts, with the necessity of increasing the density of certain events.*

Day 5 – Friday: Sub-principles and sub-sub-principles with a dominance of Velocity in the muscle contraction

This is the last of the three acquisitive days of the Morphocycle, representing a smaller fraction of playing (Silva, 2008). The configuration of this training session differs from the previous ones as competition is closer (48 hours). Complexity of the training tasks is reduced and exercises are focused on sub-principles and sub-sub-principles at inter-sectorial, sectorial and, especially, individual scales (Tamarit, 2013), leading to plenty of actions and interactions (Maciel, in Tamarit, 2013). The proximity of the next match emphasises the strategic dimension of the session, which can include situational elements in accordance with the characteristics of the following rival in competition.

Velocity is predominant on muscle activities on this day, demanding tension at the beginning of the contraction, but always with a short duration. The pauses between exercises must guarantee a discontinuous pattern, in a middle position between Wednesday (more discontinuous) and Thursday (more continuous). Tamarit (2013) highlights that exercises on this day should contain displacements at high speeds in an individual context, searching for a maximal velocity in the fibre contractions (Oliveira et al., 2007). As a major difference with training organisation on Wednesday, Friday should not include a high density of eccentric contractions, so demanding activities as jumps, landings, stops or accelerations should be removed from the drills to avoid increasing the tension.

The overall mental-emotional and physical requirements on Friday have to be lower than those from Wednesday and Thursday. This is why the number of repetitions of each exercise has to decrease. Training tasks to be included on this day can be with little (7v3, 8v4) or without opposition (5v0, 11v0), focusing on speed of execution (Tamarit, 2007; Silva, 2008). Oliveira et al. (2007) explain that one-third of action time belongs to executing a movement, whereas the remaining two-thirds are employed in perceiving and deciding. For instance, these authors believe that Friday should focus on the third of the equation which corresponds to the speed of execution. The other two-thirds, the discrimination and identification of situations, represent the tactical culture of the player and are included in the training objectives of the rest of the week, belonging to the "knowing about knowing to do" sphere which was previously explained.

Day 6 – Saturday: Recovery and Activation

The final day before a game has to be straight forward, predisposing for the next match day (Silva, 2008). At this stage, all the structural work carried out during the week has to converge in the strategic framework of competition. For instance, this day holds a double objective: ensuring recovery from the acquisitive phase of the week and activation for competition (Oliveira, in Silva, 2008).

Exercises on Saturday must have a low complexity and should be based on relevant sub-principles to remember all the tactical aspects which have been covered during the Morphocycle. This helps consolidating the dynamic automatisms of the team towards competition (Tamarit, 2007). In order to achieve the activation purpose, exercises have to contain a small dose of muscular tension and velocity in the contraction, always with a reduced density and a short duration (Tamarit, 2013).

Day 7 – Sunday: Competition

The competition establishes the temporal limit of the Morphocycle. Achieving an optimal team performance on this day is the most important objective and, as Frade (2003, in Silva, 2008) claims, competition is the best tool to control the process. Therefore, there is no better test to evaluate individual and team performances than examining if the players are able to manifest behaviour regularities in accordance with the Game Model during the official fixtures, that is, assessing if the intended specific way of playing is addressed (Silva, 2008). This competitive performance involves all the players of the team, during a 90 minute game and in a full pitch dimension. Due to the different sources of stress which wrap the competition (opponents, crowd, media, etc.) this day places the greatest emotional demands on the footballers.

As a conclusion to this section, Figure III.3 summarises the basic characteristics that should help to configure the training sessions during the Morphocycle. Silva (2008) and Tamarit (2013) represent each day of the Morphocycle with a different colour, according to its meaning. Monday (day off) is coloured in white as there is no activity on this day. The second day of the week (Tuesday) is represented by light green, obtained from the combination of competition (green) and day off (white). The first acquisitive day, Wednesday, is characterised as blue, whereas the last (Friday) is yellow. The mixture of these two days results in dark green (Thursday). Saturday aims to recover footballers from the acquisitive phase and prepare them for competition and, thus, it is represented by light yellow (yellow from Friday and white from Monday). The resulting colour of adding all of the days of the week is green, which characterises competition, equivalent to mixing white (Monday), light green (Tuesday), blue (Wednesday), dark green (Thursday), yellow (Friday) and light yellow (Saturday).

Complex Football

	Mon	Tue	Wed	Thu	Fri	Sat	Sun
	DAY OFF	ACTIVE RECOVERY	ACQUISTION	ACQUISTION	ACQUISTION	RECOVERY & ACTIVATE	MATCH
Complexity		Principles Sub-prin.	Sub-prin. S-sub-prin.	Principles Sub-prin.	Sub-prin. S-sub-prin.	Sub-prin.	Principles
Team Scale		Intersectorial Sectorial Group Individual	Intersectorial Sectorial Group Individual	Collective Intersectorial	Intersectorial Sectorial Group Individual	Collective Intersectorial	Collective
Mental-Emotional Demands		Low	Medium	High	Low-Medium	Low	Very High
Muscle Contraction							
Tension		Low	High	Medium	Low-Medium	Low-Medium	High
Duration		Very Short	Short	Medium-Long	Very Short	Very Short	Long
Velocity		Low	Medium	Low-Medium	High	Low-Medium	High
Density		Very Low	High	Medium-High	Low-Medium	Low-Medium	High
Exercise Characteristics							
Space		Medium	Small	Big	Small	Medium	Big
Time		Short-Medium	Short	Long	Short	Short-Medium	Long
Number of Players		Medium	Low	High	Low	Medium-High	High
Continuity		Very discont.	Discontinuous	Continuous	Discontinuous	Discontinuous	Continuous

Figure III.3 Basic characteristics of the Morphocycle
(after Oliveira et al., 2007; Silva, 2008; Tamarit, 2007, 2013).

III.4.3 The Exceptional Morphocycle

This kind of Morphocycle is characteristic of teams that take part in more than one official match per week. If more than 72 hours are necessary to recover from a competition match (Frade, in Tamarit, 2013) then weeks with a greater density of games severely compromises an adequate effort:recovery pattern. Therefore, there would be no time or place to organise acquisitive training sessions in these Exceptional Morphocycles, which would have as major aims to recover from the previous competition and to activate the players towards the following match.

The logistical circumstances (density of competitions, trips, number of players in the squad, etc.) play an important role in the way to organise this peculiar Morphocycle. If this type of week occasionally occurs in the season, training can be organised as shown in Figure III.4. In this modelled week there are no days off and the days immediately after a match are concerned on recovery. On the other side, when approaching the following competition interest is placed on activation and match preparation. This is why José Mourinho´s training the day before a match is based on large principles, with very little competition and working on the positioning of the team under 11v0 or 11v11 situations (Oliveira et al., 2007).

Sun	Mon	Tue	Wed	Thu	Fri	Sat	Sun
MATCH	REC.	REC. + ACT.	**MATCH**	REC.	REC.	REC. + ACT.	**MATCH**

Figure III.4 The Exceptional Morphocycle (after Tamarit, 2013).
REC: Recovery; ACT: Activation.

Inside the Exceptional Morphocycle we can identify two different sub-cycles, a shorter (three days between matches) and a longer (four days between matches). This outlook might seem banal but it is extremely important as three days between fixtures can compromise physical performance and increase injury incidence. In this respect, recent studies have shown that fixture congestion has an effect on injury rates in professional football teams (Bengtsonn *et al.*, 2013; Dellal *et al.*, 2013; Dupont *et al.*, 2010). Coaches should be especially aware of this kind of scenarios because when top-class teams add long distance travels to other countries, climate and time zone differences, national team games and other external variables to the equation, the overall fatigue (mental-emotional and physical) which the players are subjected to is dramatically elevated.

Furthermore, when Exceptional Morphocycles are consecutively repeated, as it happens in the congested match calendars characteristic of elite European teams, coaches have to include periodical days off in the course of the week to fight fatigue. In this case, it is almost mandatory to have one day off per week (or a day off every two weeks), which should be arranged the day after a match in the longer sub-cycle of the week. Tamarit (2013) recalls that under these circumstances the directional matrix of the team should be periodically reinforced, as when playing many games the footballers can forget the basics of the organisation, due to the coach not having time to implement acquisitive training sessions during the weeks. This is especially transcendent when opposition teams do not allow the manifestation of the own playing idea. In this case, the coach has to find strategies (as video analysis or theoretical explanations) to keep the playing philosophy of the team alive.

Figure III.5 shows a real competition calendar from a top-class team during a five week period (September-October 2013). For teams taking part in the UEFA Champions League, it is common that an important part of the squad is involved in international games with their home countries. When putting together the fixture list of the team and the training camps of national teams, one can get a visual idea of the competition density. During this condensed fixture periods, the team follows a series of activation for matches > competition > recovery sequences, with no additional time for acquisitive sessions.

Frade's Tactical Periodisation

Mon	Tue	Wed	Thu	Fri	Sat	Sun
INTERNATIONALS			Active Recovery	Rec.+Act. (Travel)	League (A)	Active Recovery
Rec.+Act. (Travel)	Champions League (A)	Day Off	Active Recovery	Training	Rec.+Act.	League (H)
Active Recovery	Rec.+Act. (Travel)	League (A)	Active Recovery	Rec.+Act.	League (H)	Day Off
Active Recovery	Rec.+Act.	Champions League (H)	Active Recovery	Rec.+Act. (Travel)	League (A)	Day Off
INTERNATIONALS						

Figure III.5 A five week competition period from a team taking part in the UEFA Champions League. (H) Home game; (A) Away game; Rec: Recovery; Act.: Activation.

One particular situation which is characteristic of most of the pre-seasons is having to play more than one friendly match per week. In this case, these fixtures have to be used as training sessions to improve collective organisation. Therefore, these matches can be considered as a Thursday in the habitual Morphocycle, that is, a day focused on large principles with a dominance of duration in the muscle contractions. In the first few weeks after coming back from holidays the players cannot be suddenly exposed to 90 minutes match playing times. Oliveira (in Tamarit, 2013) suggests dividing the match duration between the players of the squad, so each player takes part in 45 minutes per game. This will not allow the footballers develop excessive fatigue, continuing with their training regimen and adaptation processes during the rest of the Morphocycle.

Teams which are going to take part in two competitive matches per week during most part of their season might benefit from introducing this peculiar Exceptional Morphocycle as early as possible, trying to habituate and adapt the players to this planning structure, which is going to characterise their season.

III.5 TACTICAL PERIODISATION v TRADITIONAL TRAINING

As it has been explained in the previous sections, Tactical Periodisation cuts with traditional training schemes incorporating new algorithms to interpret the process. Viewed in these terms, the body and the mind cannot be independent from each other and Specificity and training must always be interrelated. Including tactical exercises in the course of the week does not imply following a Tactical Periodisation approach. In fact, it is rare to find a coach who does not use any kind tactical exercises to prepare a team for the competition. The main question is why, how and when are these tasks organised. Do they just represent a moment of inspiration of the coach when he was driving towards the training ground or do they belong to a wider picture of the situation?

Many coaches are skeptical about Tactical Periodisation. When do the players go to the gym? Has the player improved his VO_2max during the last month? Where are the GPSs? Is it possible to be physically fit without running around the field? Hundreds of questions of this kind arise in all debates and meetings on this training methodology. Not many coaches are able to step outside their comfort zone and investigate into new training directions. "I know that when the players run three sets of six minutes with 20/20 seconds work to rest ratio, the players are fit", is a typical statement of a fitness coach. There is no doubt that this kind of training improves the aerobic fitness of a player, but would it be more beneficial to do a 20 minutes task with appropriate tactical objectives? It is probable that many coaches lack security to implement training tasks that fully stimulate all the dimensions of the footballers. Therefore, for these coaches, it is much easier telling the players to run around the field for 20 minutes than designing a task based on tactical objectives inside a particular effort dynamic. Oliveira *et al.* (2007) carried out a detailed analysis of Portuguese First division teams training activities during the 2004-05 pre-season, revealing that not a single team prioritised tactical organisation in the initial weeks. Interestingly, a decade later, we still see a great percentage of teams including a variety of nonspecific contents in the first few weeks of the preparation period, which is the stage of the year with the greatest training time available.

One of the most crucial commandments of Tactical Periodisation is that the Game Model must precede training methodology, which implies that the coach has to generate exercises that conduct the team to behave in an expected way during the match (Mourinho, 2003, in Oliveira *et al.*, 2007). For this reason, it is not about the coach and staff copying exercises which have proven effective in other teams, but creating specific drills for each environment (Tamarit, 2013). In this sense, Frade (in Tamarit, 2013) asserts, "The coach will not do something because he once saw it, but because his intuition and reflection will show him that it is the best way to acquire the pretended principle." This guideline has to be respected since the beginning of the season, developing a pathway to direct the tactical growth of the players and the team. It is extremely important to respect this idea because when the leadership of the coach is only based on psychological variables there will only be short term effects on the performance of the team. On the other hand, the benefits of implementing a coherent training methodology are durable, as it introduces structural transformations (Mourinho, in Oliveira *et al.*, 2007).

When comparing Tactical Periodisation to other training methodologies, it is important to determine which dimension is situated as the nucleus of the process. Traditional training currents of thought have placed the physical dimension of the footballer above all the others. This means that it is imperative for the player to achieve certain physical scores (measured by match-analysis techniques or fitness tests) to take part in the game. The initial chapter of this book brought light to this topic, determining the limitations that this kind of quantitative analysis of performance had on team sports. Under the paradigm of Tactical Periodisation, quantitative performance measurements obtained by fitness tests, heart rate monitors, GPS or match analysis systems, based uniquely on the physical dimension, are of little significance. Nevertheless, this industrialised training perspective is predominant worldwide. The language employed by coaches and journalist when referring to the game does not help to break down these barriers as terms like work, effort, load, sweat or war belong to the usual jargon. Altogether, it seems in many times that success is not about how good the player produces, but instead on how much he produces.

Mourinho (in Oliveira *et al.*, 2007) has been critical with this physicalisation of performance as he believes football and footballers are global, with an interaction between all the dimensions. Therefore, Mourinho (2005, in Oliveira *et al.*, 2007) feels unable to dissociate between physical, technical, tactical and psychological aspects ensuring that:

> *The [sporting] shape is not physical. The shape is much more than that. The physical side is the least significant for the consecution of the sporting shape. Without organisation and talent to explore a system of play, deficiencies are more visible, but they do not have to do with the physical shape.*

For instance, being in a good shape has more to do with playing collectively inside a Game Model rather than with individual manifestations of physical parameters: covering more distance at high-intensities or sprinting a greater number of times. Faria (2003, in Oliveira *et al.*, 2007) supports this statement by arguing, "The physical side is highly overrated despite the game organisation being essential. The secret is in knowing to be, knowing to do." Altogether, football is not about being in a good or bad physical shape, it is about being adapted to a way of playing (Mourinho, in Oliveira *et al.*, 2007).

Tactical Periodisation ignores analytical exercises for the development of any dimension in isolation. Moreover, there are no complementary exercises dedicated to physical capacities like strength, endurance or speed, as these have to be related to the way the team plays (Oliveira *et al.*, 2007). All the dimensions have to be developed in Specificity during the training sessions. This also means that the traditional fitness coach will have an entirely different role and outlook in Tactical Periodisation. Instead of being concerned on independently developing physical capacities, he will be in charge of creating tasks which lead to improve the acquisition of the principles of the Game Model of the team (Mourinho, 2004, in Oliveira *et al.*, 2007).

Another football methodology —integrated training— has become popular in the last few years as it has been based on introducing the ball to develop physical capacities, trying to provide a more systemic perspective of the process. As an example, under a traditional training prism, aerobic power could be improved by running four sets of four minutes around a football field at a running speed where the heart rate exceeds 85% of its maximal values (Helgerud *et al.*, 2001). With the same physiological aim, an integrated training drill could be a 5v5 small sided game with supporting players in the outside of the field of play (Hoff *et al.*, 2002). As the physiological response during both kinds of drills is very similar, given that the same work to rest ratios are respected (Impellizzeri *et al.*, 2006), and players are more motivated when the ball is present in training, many coaches have decided in favour of this integral training method.

However, it should be highlighted that Tactical Periodisation diverges from integrated training, as in the latter the physical dimension governs the action (Oliveira, in Tamarit, 2007). Integrated training uses the ball to disguise physical training, but the final aim is the development of physical capacities. This is a critical difference with Tactical Periodisation, where the training exercises are never focused on abstract physical capacities but on acquiring a certain way of play (Mourinho, in Oliveira *et al.*, 2007), with the tactical supra-dimension in charge of leading the process.

An additional key difference between Tactical Periodisation and the conventional football methodologies is the role given to gym-based strength programs. Rui Faria (in Oliveira *et al.*, 2007) questions himself how can synergies be identified between muscular development using body-building machines and the requirements of a certain Game Model. Mourinho (in Oliveira *et al.*, 2007) corroborates this by asserting:

> *I do not use individual body building programs with my players to maintain or potentiate certain qualities. I do not believe in this. What I do is related to our Game Model. The gym and body-building machines are for the medical department, if they think they are useful in the rehabilitation from injuries.*

At this point, some readers might argue that without gym training footballers could experience a higher injury risk. However, if we examine injury statistics from the last decade (as those from UEFA Champions League research projects) we can observe that teams managed by José Mourinho do not have a great amount of non-traumatic injuries in the course of the season. Again, Mourinho (in Oliveira *et al.*, 2007) believes this is not by chance as:

Training plays a crucial role: the more specific the work has been, the more prepared will the muscle be for effort and for the season. This is something evident, pragmatic and basic. What is the best for the muscle? The actions that we call 'technical-strength', tactical-technical actions carried out at very high intensities and elevated speeds. For example, stopping after a physical contact and a change of direction with a sprint is a 'strength' action much more specific that a 200 kg leg press. For this reason, the muscle is much more prepared and adapted to effort when working this way. Sometimes people are obsessed with the physical side, considering the muscle as a work generator organ and not as a sensible organ, with a fantastic capacity to adapt to a regular development.

From all of the above, the best way to clarify and conclude this chapter is with the following statement from Oliveira *et al.* (2007):

Physical training, aerobic work as a basis in pre-season, the volume-intensity binomial, exercises arranged in circuits and stations, conjunct training, friendly games in the middle of the week, gym, fitness tests, medicine balls, visiting the city park, running with or without the ball around the field, shorter games to assess endurance, etc. are things totally away from Mourinho´s method, in both pre-season and competition.

EPILOGUE

"We will never have a total knowledge"

Edgar Morin

This book has tried to provide a different way to see, study and examine football, presenting two different training methodologies: Structured Training and Tactical Periodisation. However, these two contemporary philosophies must not be considered antagonistic but complementary, as the similarities are greater than the differences between them. Josep Mussons, former FC Barcelona vice-president, illustrates the following anecdote back from the year 1996 to enhance the consensus of viewpoints (in Suárez, 2012):

> *I recall perfectly that day. It was 3 p.m. when I received Robson [Sir Bobby Robson] and Mourinho in my office. Núñez and Gaspart [at that time FC Barcelona´s president and vice-president, respectively] had promised the new manager to host him in a house at Sitges, so they took him rapidly there. Mourinho stayed in my office. Paco Seirul·lo (responsible of fitness training in Barcelona and an academic institution in training theory) came in. They both started to talk incessantly, seated on the couch for more than two hours, about very precise technical and tactical questions. Mourinho insisted that training should change, as not everybody should be running round the field; some of them could need it but others would not. Seirul·lo admitted his knowledge was notable. Even with Helenio Herrera I did not have such a good time.*

Capra (1996) anticipated many of the statements which have been presented along the preceding pages and claimed that the major problems of our era "cannot be understood in isolation." Thus, the purpose of this book was not to divide but to multiply, allowing the reader to explore and emerge new directions in football training. Nevertheless, we have to respect that in this search for innovative strategies and alternatives to conceive football and nature, we will always find many obstacles in our way. Even top-class managers as Pep Guardiola reflect the uncertainties of applying a novel training methodology in a different culture and, after being praised for using the ball since an early stage during his first pre-season at Bayern, alerted (in Perarnau, 2014):

> *Yes, that's great, but if we lose two games in a row they will say it is because of the rondos and because we are not doing 1000 meters running sets during the pre-season or because we did not climbed mountains in the Trentino.*

Our previous learning story is another of the most anchored barriers we have to overcome, as our brain is the first one to trick us (Rubia, 2007). We are predisposed to perceive what we really want to perceive, so we need to change the level of analysis to see things that previously could not be seen (Punset, 2004, in Pol, 2011). Even though Classical Thinking remains in the foundations of football, the general systems theory and complexity sciences have yielded concepts, models and tools to understand football in a more adequate way: the player as a functional unit in Structured Training and the game as an indivisible reality in Tactical Periodisation. Hence, Seirul·lo's is concerned on the footballer as a system, focusing on the self-structuring and optimising processes in the person, whereas Frade gives priority to the team as a system, concentrating on its organisation and the game dynamics. Talking in Seirul·lo's terms, Frade's view could be defined as tactical prioritisation or tactical optimisation.

Paco Seirul·lo and Vítor Frade have to be considered among the greatest football thinkers and influencers of our era, having produced a magnificent job to set the foundations of this new vision of the footballer and of football. They both concurred that the classical approximation to study team sports based on individual sports did not satisfied the singularity of football and, thus, investigated for new strategies, confronting the doctrinal pragmatic knowledge spread throughout the universe of football. For instance, during many years, they fought great cultural reminiscences which still, in our days, form part of the unconscious plane of many coaches.

Epliogue

Not only have Seirul·lo and Frade supported their methodologies in a profound theoretical background, but also have contrasted their postulates in top-class football scenarios, which have enriched the quality of their proposals. Success at team level gave them the substantial strength to combat the obstacles which they found on their way. Many of these were represented by sceptic people who asked for certainties in a sport formed by not demonstrable predictions. Basing training on the brain and not on the muscle, conceiving it as a nonlinear and creative process where coaches are able to generate infinite proposals and the weekly organisation design (Structured Microcycle and Morphocycle, respectively), remain as fundamental analogies between methodologies.

From here on, it is up to every coach to continue developing his personal training pathway as, according to Edgar Morin and the Paradigm of Complexity, knowledge is a dynamic and incomplete process (Morin, 1994).

BIBLIOGRAPHY

- Álvaro, J. (2002). Modelos de planificación y programación en deportes de equipo. Master en Alto Rendimiento Deportivo. Madrid (Spain): Comité Olímpico Español-Universidad Autónoma de Madrid.

- Álvaro, J., Badillo, J.J., González, J.L., Navarro, F., Portolés, J., Sánchez, F. (1995). Modelo de análisis de los deportes colectivos basado en el rendimiento en la competición. Infocoes, I, 21-40.

- Araújo, D., Davids, K., Hristovski, R. (2006). The ecological dynamics of decision making in sport. Psychology of Sports and Exercise, 7, 653-676.

- Arjol, J.L. (2012). La planificación actual del entrenamiento en el fútbol: Análisis comparado del enfoque estructurado y la periodización táctica. Acción Motriz, 8, 27-37.

- Ascensão, A., Leite, M., Rebelo, A.N., Magalhäes, S., Magalhäes, J. (2011). Effects of cold water immersion on the recovery of physical performance and muscle damage following a one-off soccer match. Journal of Sports Sciences, 29, 217-225.

- Balagué, N., Torrents, C. (2011). Complejidad y deporte. Barcelona (Spain): Inde.

- Balagué, N., Torrents, C. (2014). Aceptar la complejidad en el fútbol: Una tarea compleja. In P. Gómez (ed.): El fútbol ¡no! es así, pp. 182-185. Barcelona (Spain): Fútbol de libro.

- Balagué, N., Torrents, C., Hristovski, R., Davids, K., Araújo, D. (2013). Overview of complex systems in sports. Journal of System Science and Complexity, 26, 4-13.

- Baldari, C., Videira, M., Madeira, F., Sergio, J., Guidetti, L. (2004). Lactate removal during active recovery related to the individual anaerobic and ventilatory thresholds in soccer players. European Journal of Applied Physiology, 93, 224-230.

- Bangsbo, J. (1994). The physiology of soccer – with special reference to intense intermittent exercise. Acta Physiologica Scandinavica, 151 Suppl. 619.

- Bayer, C. (1986). La enseñanza de los juegos deportivos colectivos. Barcelona (Spain): Hispano Europea.

- Bengtsson, H., Ekstrand, J., Hägglund, M. (2013). Muscle injury rates in professional football increase with fixture congestion: an 11-year follow-up of the UEFA Champions League injury study. British Journal of Sports Medicine, 47, 743-747.

- Berstein, N. (1967). The co-ordination and regulation of movement. London (UK): Pergamon Press.

- Bloomfield, J., Polman, R., O′Donoghue, P. (2007). Physical demands of different positions in FA Premier League soccer. Journal of Science and Medicine in Sport, 6, 63-70.

- Bompa, T. (1984). Theory and methodology of training – The key to athletic performance. Florida (USA): Kendal/Hunt.

- Bondarchuk, A.P. (1988). Constructing a training system. Track Technique, 102, 254-269.

- Bondarchuk, A.P. (2007). Transfer of training in sport. Volume I. Michigan (USA): Ultimate Athlete Concepts.

- Borasteros, D. (2005). El "pinganillo" de Raúl. El País (Spain), 24 August.

- Bradley, P.S., Sheldon, W., Wooster, B., Olsen, P., Boanas, P., Krustrup. P. (2009). High-intensity running in English FA Premier League soccer matches. Journal of Sports Sciences, 27, 159-168.

- Campos, C. (2007). A singularidade da intervençao do treinador como a sua "Impressao Digital" na… Justificaçao da Periodizaçao Táctica como uma "fenomenotécnica". Monograph. Faculdade de Desporto da Universidad do Porto (Portugal).

- Cano, O. (2009). El modelo de juego del FCBarcelona. (Third Edition). Vigo (Spain): MC Sports.

- Cano, O. (2012). El juego de posición del FC Barcelona. Vigo (Spain): MC Sports.

- Cappa, A. (2007). La preparación física no existe. Interview with Paco Seirul·lo. Marca (Spain), 24 November.

- Capra, F. (1996). The web of life. London (UK): Harper Collins Publishers.

- Castelo, J. (1999). Fútbol. Estructura y dinámica de juego. Barcelona (Spain): INDE.

- Damasio, A.R. (1996). El error de Descartes. Santiago (Chile): Andrés Bello.(1

- Dellal, A., Chamari, K., Wong, D.P., Ahmaidi, S., Keller, D., Barros, R., Bisciotti, G.N., Carling, C. (2011). Comparison of physical and technical performance in European soccer match-play: FA Premier League and La Liga. European Journal of Sports Sciences, 11, 51-59.

- Dellal, A., Lago-Peñas, C., Rey, E., Chamari, K., Orhant, E. (2013). The effects of a congested fixture period on physical performance, technical activity and injury rate during matches in a professional soccer team. British Journal of Sports Medicine. doi:10.1136/bjsports-2012-091290.

- Díaz, J.M. (2011). Seirul·lo, la gasolina del rondo. Sport (Spain), 26 June.

- Dick, F. (1980). Sport training principles. London (UK): Lepus Books.

- Di Salvo, V., Baron, R., Tschan, H., Callejon Montero, F.J., Bachl, N., Pigozzi, F. (2007). Performance characteristics according to playing position in elite soccer. International Journal of Sports Medicine, 28, 222-227.

- Domenech, O. (2013). En los rondos, Valdés era mejor que yo. Interview with Gianluca Zambrotta. El Mundo Deportivo (Spain), 19 February.

- Duarte, R., Araújo, D., Correia, V., Davids, K. (2012). Sport teams as superorganisms: Implications of sociobiological models of behaviour for research and practice in team sports performance analysis. Sports Medicine, 42, 633-642.

- Duarte, R., Araújo, D., Correia, V., Davids, K., Marques, P., Richardson, M.J. (2013). Competing together: Assessing the dynamics of team-team and player-team synchrony in professional association football. Human Movement Science, 32, 555-566.

- Dupont, G., Nedelec, M., McCall, A., McCormack, D., Berthoin, S., Wisloff, U. (2010). Effect of 2 soccer matches in a week on physical performance and injury rate. American Journal of Sports Medicine, 38, 1752-1758.

- Ekblom, B. (1986). Applied physiology of soccer. Sports Medicine, 3, 50-60.

- Frank, T.D., Richardson, M.J. (2010). On a test static for the Kuramoto order parameter of synchronization: An illustration for group synchronization during rocking chairs. Physica D, 239, 2084-2092.

- Freedman, D.H. (2010). Wrong: Why experts keep failing us. New York (USA): Little, Brown and Company.

- García Manso, J.M. (1999). Alto rendimiento, la adaptación y la excelencia deportiva. Madrid (Spain): Gymnos.

- Garganta, J. (1997). Para una teoría de los juegos deportivos colectivos. In A. Graça, J. Oliveira (eds.): La enseñanza de los juegos deportivos, pp. 9-23. Barcelona (Spain): Paidotribo.

- Gibson, J.J. (1979). The ecological approach to visual perception. USA: Houghton Mifflin.

- Gómez, P. (2009). Messi tiene talento para ciertas cosas, lo demás es construido. Interview with Paco Seirul·lo. La Voz de Galicia (Spain), 8 May.

- González Badillo, J.J. (2002) Métodos de analysis de la exigencia de la condición física en los deportes. Master in High Peformance in Sport. Autónoma University of Madrid. Spanish Olympic Committee.

- Gregson, W., Drust, B., Atkinson, G., Di Salvo, V. (2010). Match-to-match variability of high-speed activities in Premier League soccer. International Journal of Sports Medicine, 31, 237-242.

- Greháigne, J.F. (2001). La organización del juego en el fútbol. Barcelona (Spain): Inde.

- Greháigne, J.F., Davis, K., Bennet, S., Button, C. (1997). Dynamic-system analysis of opponent relationships in collective actions in soccer. Journal of Sports Sciences, 15, 137-149.

- Haken, H. (1983). Synergetic, an introduction. Berlin (Germany): Springer.

- Harre, D. (1973). Trainingslehre. Berlin (Germany): Sportverlag.

- Hay, J.G. & Reid, J.G. (1982). Anatomy mechanics and human motion. New Jersey (USA): Prentice-Hall.

- Hegedüs, J. (1988). La ciencia del entrenamiento deportivo. Buenos Aires (Argentina): Stadium.

- Helgerud, J., Engen, L.C., Wisloff, U., Hoff, J. (2001). Aerobic endurance training improves soccer performance. Medicine and Science in Sports and Exercise, 33, 1925-1931.

- Hernández Moreno, J. (1994). Análisis de las estructuras del juego deportivo. Barcelona (Spain): Inde.

- Hernández Moreno, J. (2001). Análisis de los parámetros espacio y tiempo en el fútbol sala. La distancia recorrida, el ritmo y la dirección de los desplazamientos del jugador en la competición. Apunts: Educación Física y Deportes, 65, 32-44.

- Hoff, J. (2005). Training and testing physical capacity for elite soccer players. Journal of Sports Sciences, 23, 573-582.

- Hoff, J., Wisloff, U., Engen, L.C., Kemi, O.J., Helgerud, J. (2002). Soccer specific aerobic endurance training. British Journal of Sports Medicine, 36, 218-221.

- Impellizzeri, F.M., Marcora, S.M., Castagna, C., Reilly, T., Sassi, A., Iaia, M., Rampinini, E. (2006). Physiological and performance effects of generic versus specific aerobic training in soccer players. International Journal of Sports Medicine, 27, 483-492.

- Issurin, V. (2008). Block periodisation versus traditional training: a review. Journal of Sports Medicine and Physical Fitness, 48, 65-75.

- Issurin, V. (2010). New horizons for the methodology and physiology of training organisation. Sports Medicine, 40, 189-206.

- Issurin, V. (2012). Entrenamiento deportivo. Periodización en bloques. Barcelona (Spain): Paidotribo.

- Kelso, J.A.S. (1995). Dynamic patterns – The self-organisation of brain behaviour. Cambridge (UK): E & MIT Press.

- King, I. (2000). Foundations of physical preparation. King Sports International.

- Kinugasa, T., Kilding, A.E. (2009). A comparison of post-match recovery strategies in youth soccer players. Journal of Strength and Conditioning Research, 23, 1402-1407.

- Kitano, H., Asada, M. (2002). RoboCup: La copa robótica mundial de fútbol. Investigación y Ciencia, 312.

- Konig, J.P. (2009). Training athletes and explaining the past in Philostratus' Gymnasticus. In E. Bowie & J. Elsner (eds), Philostratus. Greek culture in the Roman world, pp. 251-283. Cambridge (UK): Cambridge University Press.

- Krustrup, P., Mohr, M., Amstrup, T., Rysgaard, T., Johansen, J., Steensberg, A., Pedersen, P.K., Bangsbo, J. (2003). The yo-yo intermittent recovery test: physiological response, reliability and validity. Medicine and Science in Sports and Exercise, 35, 697-705.

- Krustrup, P., Mohr, M., Nybo, L., Jensen, J.M., Nielsen, J.J., Bangsbo, J. (2006). The Yo-yo IR2 test: physiological response, reliability and application to elite soccer. Medicine and Science in Sports and Exercise, 38, 1666-1673.

- Kuhn, T. (1962). The structure of scientific revolutions. Chicago (IL, USA): University of Chicago Press.

- Lago, C. (2002). La preparación física en el fútbol. Madrid (Spain): Biblioteca Nueva.

- Lago, C. (2009). La aportación de Paco Seirul·lo al conocimiento científico de los deportes de equipo. Revista de Entrenamiento Deportivo, XXIII, 4, 11-12.

- Lames, M., Ertmer, J., Walter, F. (2010). Oscillations in football - Order and disorder in spatial interactions between the two teams. International Journal of Sports Psychology, 41, 85-86.

- Lévi-Strauss, C. (1998). Las estructuras fundamentales del parentesco. Barcelona (Spain): Paidós Ibérica.

- Mahlo, F. (1969). La acción táctica en juego. La Habana (Cuba): Pueblo y Educación.

- Mallo, J. (2013). La preparación (física) para el fútbol basada en el Juego. Barcelona (Spain): Futboldlibro.

- Martín Acero, R. (2009). Paco Seirul·lo: Enhorabuena y muchas gracias! Revista de Entrenamiento Deportivo, XXIII, 4, 5-6.

- Martín Acero, R., Lago, C. (2005a). Deportes de equipo. Comprender la complejidad para elevar el rendimiento. Barcelona (Spain): INDE.

- Martín Acero, R., Lago, C. (2005b). Complejidad y rendimiento en deportes sociomotores de equipo (DSEQ): dificultades de investigación. Revista digital efdeportes.com, 90.

- Martín Acero, R., Seirul·lo, F., Lago, C., Lalín, C. (2013). Causas objetivas de la planificación en DSEQ (II): La Microestructura (microciclos). Revista de Entrenamiento Deportivo, 27 (2).

- Maslow, A.H. (1966). The psychology of science. Chapel Hill (NC, USA): Maurice Basset Publishing.

- Matveiev, L.P. (1964). Problem of periodisation the sport training. Moscow (Russia): Fizkultura i Sport.

- Matveiev, L.P. (1977). Periodización del entrenamiento deportivo. Madrid (Spain): Instituto Nacional de Educación Física.

- Matveiev, L.P. (1982). El proceso de entrenamiento deportivo. Buenos Aires (Argentina): Stadium.

- Matveiev, L.P. (1985). Fundamentos del entrenamiento deportivo. Madrid (Spain): Esteban Sanz.

- McGarry, T., Anderson, D., Wallace, S., Hughes, M., Franks, I. (2002). Sport competition as a dynamical self-organizing system. Journal of Sports Sciences, 20, 171-181.

- Miranda, J. (2009). Organizaçao estructural: ponto de partida ou um meio para atingir um fim (o modelo de jogo)? Monograph. Faculdade de Desporto da Universidad do Porto (Portugal).

- Mohr, M., Krustrup, P., Bangsbo, J. (2003). Match performance of high-standard soccer players with special relevance to development of fatigue. Journal of Sports Sciences, 21, 519-528.

- Mombaerts, E. (1998). Fútbol. Entrenamiento y rendimiento colectivo. Barcelona (Spain): Hispano Europea.

- Monzó, J. (2006). El pensador sistémico. Volumen I. Artículos 1995-2005. Valencia (Spain).

- Morenilla, J. (2013). Francia olvidó la humildad. Interview with Lilian Thuram. El País (Spain), 23 March.

- Morin, E. (1993). El método I. La naturaleza de la naturaleza. Madrid (Spain): Cátedra.

- Morin, E. (1994). Introducción al pensamiento complejo. Barcelona (Spain): Gedisa.

- Morin, E. (2000). La mente bien ordenada. Barcelona (Spain): Seix Barral.

- Mujika, I. (2013). The alphabet of sport science research starts with q. International Journal of Sports Physiology and Performance, 8, 465-466.

- Navarro, F. (1997). Theory and Practice of sporting training. Faculty of Physical Activity and Sport Sciences. Technical University of Madrid (Spain).

- O´Connor, J. & McDermott, I. (1997). The art of systems thinking: Essential skills for creativity and problem solving. USA: Thorsons.

- Oliveira, J.G. (2003). Organiçao do jogo de uma equipa de Futebol. Aspectos metodológicos na abordagem da sua organiçao estructural e funcional. Faculdade de Desporto da Universidad do Porto (Portugal).

- Oliveira, J.G. (2004). Conhecimento Específico em Futebol. Contributos para a definiçao de una matriz dinamica do processo de ensino-aprendizagem/treino do jogo. Faculdade de Desporto da Universidad do Porto (Portugal).

- Oliveira, J.G. (2007). FC Porto: Nuestro microciclo semanal (Morfociclo). 6th Clinic on Youth Football. Pamplona (Spain): Fundación Osasuna.

- Oliveira, B., Amieiro, N., Resende, N., Barreto, R. (2007). Mourinho ¿Por qué tantas victorias? Vigo (Spain): MC Sports.

- Ozolin, N.G. (1970). The modern system of sport training. Moscow (Russia): Fizkultura I Sport.

- Palomo, F. (2012). La metodología que marcó época. Interview with Paco Seirul·lo. ESPN sports.

- Panzeri, D. (1967). Fútbol. Dinámica de lo impensado (Re-edited in 2011). Madrid (Spain): Capitán Swing Libros.

- Parlebas, P. (1988). Elementos de sociología del deporte. Málaga (Spain): Unisport, Junta de Andalucía/Universidad Internacional del Deporte de Andalucía.

- Parlebas, P. (2001). Léxico de praxiología motriz. Barcelona (Spain): Paidotribo.

- Passos, P. (2008). Dynamical decision making in rugby: Identifying interpersonal coordination patterns. Doctoral Thesis. Technical University of Lisbon (Portugal).

- Passos, P., Davids, K., Araújo, D., Paz, N., Minguéns, J., Mendes, J. (2011). Networks as a novel tool for studying team ball sports as complex social systems. Journal of Science and Medicine in Sport, 2, 170-176.

- Perarnau, M. (2014). Herr Pep. Barcelona (Spain): Córner.

- Platonov, V.N. (1988). El entrenamiento deportivo. Teoría y Metodología. Barcelona (Spain): Paidotribo.

- Pol, R. (2011). La preparación ¿física? en el fútbol. Vigo (Spain): MC Sports.

- Prigogine, I. (1993). Las leyes del caos. Barcelona (Spain): Crítica Grijalbo Mondadori.

- Punset, E. (2007). Viaje a la felicidad. Barcelona (Spain): Destino.

- Punset, E. (2010). Viaje a las emociones. Barcelona (Spain): Destino.

- Rampinini, E., Coutts, A.J., Castagna, C., Sassi, R., Impellizzeri, F.M. (2007). Variation in top level soccer match performance. International Journal of Sports Medicine, 28, 1018-1024.

- Ribeiro, J.M., Viana, A. (2013). Interview with André Villas-Boas. O Jogo (Portugal). 24th June 2013.

- Richardson, M.J, García, A., Frank, T.D., Gergor, M., Marsh, K.L. (2012). Measuring group synchrony: A cluster-phase method for analyzing multivariate movement time-series. Frontiers in Physiology, 3, 405.

- Roca, A. (2009). El proceso de entrenamiento en el fútbol. Metodología de trabajo en un equipo profesional (FC Barcelona). Vigo (Spain): MC Sports.

- Rubia, F.J. (2007). El cerebro nos engaña. Barcelona (Spain): Temas de Hoy.

- Ruíz Pérez, L.M. (1994). Deporte y aprendizaje. Madrid (Spain): Visor.

- Salebe, A. (2011). Estar en el Barça es disfrutar continuamente. Interview with Paco Seirul·lo. El Heraldo (Colombia), 20 August.

- Sampedro, J. (1999). Fundamentos de táctica deportiva. Análisis de la estrategia en los deportes. Madrid (Spain): Gymnos.

- Schmidt, R.A. (1982). Motor control and learning. A behavioural emphasis. Champaign (IL, USA): Human Kinetics.

- Seirul·lo, F. (1976). Hacia una sinergética del entrenamiento. Apuntes Medicina Deporte, XIII, 50, 93-94.

- Seirul·lo, F. (1979). Desarrollo de las cualidades físicas básicas. Atletismo Español, August, 37-39 & November, 25-29.

- Seirul·lo, F. (1986). Entrenamiento coadyuvante. Apunts de Medicina Esportiva, 23, 38-41.

- Seirul·lo, F. (1987a). Opciones de planificación en los deportes de largo período de competiciones. Revista de Entrenamiento Deportivo, I (3), 53-62.

- Seirul·lo, F. (1987b). Las funciones y competencias de un preparador físico en un club deportivo. Revista de Entrenamiento Deportivo, I (1), 70-77.

- Seirul·lo, F. (1987c). La técnica y su entrenamiento. Apunts Medicina de l'Esport, 24, 189-199.

- Seirul·lo, F. (1990). Entrenamiento de la fuerza en balonmano. Revista de Entrenamiento Deportivo, IV, 6, 30-34.

- Seirul·lo, F. (1993). Planificación del entrenamiento en deportes de equipo. Máster en Alto Rendimiento Deportivo. Módulo 2.1.7. Madrid (Spain): Comité Olímpico Español – Universidad Autónoma de Madrid.

- Seirul·lo, F. (1998a). Planificación a largo plazo en los deportes colectivos. Curso sobre entrenamiento Deportivo en la infancia y la adolescencia. Escuela Canaria del Deporte. Dirección General de Deportes del Gobierno de Canarias.

- Seirul·lo, F. (1998b). Prólogo. In G. Cometti: La pliometría. Barcelona (Spain): INDE.

- Seirul·lo, F. (1999). Criterios modernos de entrenamiento en el fútbol. Revista Training Fútbol, 45, 8-17.

- Seirul·lo, F. (2000). Una línea de trabajo distinta. I Jornadas de Actualización de Preparadores Físicos de fútbol. Comité Olímpico Español.

- Seirul·lo, F. (2001). Entrevista de metodología y planificación. Training Fútbol, 65, 8-17.

- Seirul·lo, F. (2002). La preparación física en deportes de equipo. Entrenamiento Estructurado. Jornada sobre Rendimiento Deportivo. Dirección General del Deporte. Valencia (Spain).

- Seirul·lo, F. (2003). Sistemas dinámicos y rendimiento en deportes de equipo. First Meeting of Complex Systems and Sports. Instituto Nacional de Educació Física de Catalunya. Barcelona (Spain).

- Seirul·lo, F. (2004). Motricidad básica y su aplicación a la iniciación deportiva. Instituto Nacional de Educación Física de Catalunya (Spain).

- Seirul·lo, F. (2005a). Prologo. In R. Martín Acero, C. Lago: Deportes de equipo. Comprender la complejidad para elevar el rendimiento. Barcelona (Spain): INDE.

- Seirul·lo, F. (2005b). Planificación del entrenamiento. Máster profesional en Alto Rendimiento en deportes de equipo. Barcelona (Spain): CEDE.

- Seirul·lo, F. (2005c). Estructura socio-afectiva. Máster profesional en Alto Rendimiento en deportes de equipo. Barcelona (Spain): CEDE.

- Seirul·lo, F. (2009). Una línea de trabajo distinta. Revista de Entrenamiento Deportivo, XXIII, 4, 13-18.

- Seirul·lo, F. (2012). Competencias: Desde la Educación Física al Alto Rendimiento. Revista de Education Física, 128, 5-8.

- Silva, M. (2008). O desenvolvimento do jogar, segundo a Periodizaçao Táctica. Pontevedra (Spain): MC Sports.

- Siff, M.C., Verkhoshansky, Y. (2000). Superentrenamiento. Badalona (Spain): Paidotribo.

- Solé, J. (2002). Fundamentos del entrenamiento deportivo. Barcelona (Spain): Ergo.

- Sousa, P.D. (2009). Un algoritmo do FUTBOL (mais do que) TOTAL: algo que lhe dá o Ritmo. Uma reflexao sobre o "jogar" de qualidade. Monograph. Faculdade de Desporto da Universidad do Porto (Portugal).

- Stolen, T., Chamari, K., Castagna, C., Wisloff, U. (2005). Physiology of soccer: An update. Sports Medicine, 35, 501-536.

- Suárez, O. (2009). Hablamos de fútbol. You First Foundation. El Mundo (Spain).

- Suárez, O. (2012). Palabra de entrenador (2nd Edition). Barcelona (Spain): Editorial Corner.

- Tamarit, X. (2007). ¿Qué es la Periodización Táctica? Vivenciar el juego para condicionar el Juego. Vigo (Spain): MC Sports.

- Tamarit, X. (2013). Periodización Táctica v Periodización Táctica. Spain: MBF.

- Tassara, H., Pila, A. (1986). Guía práctica del entrenador de fútbol. Madrid (Spain): Augusto E. Pila Teleña.

- Tavares, J. (2013). Tactical Periodisation. Periodisation Expert Meeting. London (UK), 19th-23rd June 2013. World Football Academy.

- Torrents, C. (2005). La teoría de los sistemas dinámicos y el entrenamiento deportivo. Doctoral thesis. Universitat de Barcelona: Institut Nacional d'Educació Física de Catalunya.

- Tshciene, P. (2002). Algunos aspectos de la preparación a la competición. La preparación a la competición según un enfoque basado en la teoría de los sistemas. Revista de Entrenamiento Deportivo, 4, 5-15.

- Verheijen, R. (2013). Periodisation in Football. One day periodisation course. Wolverhampton (UK), 18 February.

- Verkhoshansky, Y. (1990). Entrenamiento deportivo, planificación y programación. Barcelona (Spain): Martínez Roca.

- Verkhoshansky, Y. & Verkhosansky, N. (2011). Special strength training manual for coaches. Rome (Italy): Verkhoshansky SSTM.

- Vila, J. (2012). La organización de la cantera del FC Barcelona. II Jornadas sobre el trabajo de las canteras en el fútbol. Seville (Spain). 29 December.

- Wilson, J. (2013). Inverting the pyramid: The history of football tactics (Second edition). London (UK): Orion.

- Yue, Z., Broich, H., Seifriz, F., MEster, J. (2008). Mathematical analysis of a soccer game. Part I: Individual and collective behaviours. Studies in Applied Mathematics, 121, 223-243.